YOUTH

John Buckeridge is the Executive Editor of *YOUTHWORK* magazine. He is the author of the popular *Ready To Use Meeting Guide* series (Kingsway) and *Nurturing Young Disciples* (HarperCollins).

John Allan is the Senior Youth Worker at Belmont Chapel, Exeter. He is the author of over twenty books and is a Consulting Editor of *YOUTHWORK* magazine.

Danny Brierley is Youth and Children's Director at Altrincham Baptist Church where he is responsible for over 200 young people and 60 volunteer workers.

Steve Chalke is a preacher, Baptist minister, television presenter, and International Director of Oasis Trust. He is a prolific writer of books and magazine articles.

Andy Hickford is the Pastor of Maybridge Christian Fellowship, Worthing, West Sussex, and a Consulting Editor of *YOUTHWORK* magazine.

Youthwork Handbook

JOHN BUCKERIDGE

WITH JOHN ALLAN, DANNY BRIERLEY,
STEVE CHALKE AND ANDY HICKFORD

KINGSWAY PUBLICATIONS
EASTBOURNE

First Published 1996

Cover photo: Jonathan Mark/Brainstormers

Design: Rachel Salter

ISBN 0 85476 625 1

Produced by Bookprint Creative Services
P.O. Box 827, BN21 3YJ, England for
KINGSWAY PUBLICATIONS LTD
Lottbridge Drove, Eastbourne, E. Sussex BN23 6NT.
Printed in Great Britain.

Contents

This book has two distinct halves.

Section one contains ten introductory chapters on youth ministry. These look at some of the basics that will help provide a good foundation for your youth work.

Section two contains the names and addresses of hundreds of full-time youth workers, denominational youth officers, youth ministry organisations, residential centres and a listing of useful youth ministry resources. It is impossible to be completely comprehensive with any type of directory, but I hope this directory will aid networking between local full-time and volunteer youth workers and resourcing people and agencies. It also includes details of some of the alternative worship/youth congregations which are springing up all over the UK.

While reasonable efforts have been made to ensure the accuracy of the various entries in the directory at the time of going to print, information may change. The author and publishers do not accept any liability for loss or damage of any kind which may arise from an error or omission of any entry. Entries are provided free of charge and at the discretion of the author.

If you or your organisation are not included, and you feel you should be, drop me a line at the address below with your name and address. If, as planned, we produce an updated directory in the future, I'll be in touch.

John Buckeridge, YOUTHWORK, 37 Elm Road, New Malden, Surrey KT3 3HB.

Section One

AN INTRODUCTION TO YOUTH MINISTRY

Chapter One

KEY TRENDS IN YOUTH MINISTRY

by John Buckeridge

I wished I was somewhere else. Lloyd had sat on the bonnet of the car and was refusing to get off, even though the very irate driver was revving the engine. With all his mates egging him on, Lloyd grabbed the wipers and held on for dear life. Meanwhile the driver, red-faced and swearing, was making the car kangaroo-hop across the pub car park in an effort to dislodge the mildly drunk sixteen-year-old. Someone had to do something. I prayed, took a deep breath and was about to step forward.

Suddenly the car was gone – in a cloud of fumes – and Lloyd was left intact, standing beside me.

Meeting Lloyd and his friends by the fish and chip shop, or wherever else they happened to be on Tuesday nights, was always unpredictable. The previous fortnight had included an incident with a foam fire extinguisher at the petrol station and a food fight with stolen cakes.

In eight years of detached youth work I often felt like a UN peace-keeper instead of a youth worker from my church. And yet, peace-keeping, mediating and 'being there' amid the boredom, pain and dislocation which mark the lives of so many young people today is surely what Christ calls us to do. This does, however, require a sense of call.

Knowing that God wants you to be involved in youth ministry is important. It provides impetus to continue when the disappointments wash over you like large, cold waves. And disappointments will be no

stranger to anyone who really gets involved in the lives of young people – it's the nature of the task. But, despite the many and inevitable lows, youth ministry in the 1990s is increasingly exciting.

In my opinion there are presently six key trends in youth ministry which are particularly shaping the thinking of Christian youth workers. Together they make this period of British church history a very challenging time for anyone serious about youth ministry.

1. A sense of urgency

Statistics from church surveys have shown that we are failing to effectively reach and keep young people. After decades of declining numbers, many churches are waking up to the realisation that something must be done to attract and hold on to children and young people. This new sense of urgency has resulted in a range of responses. In some churches more money has been channelled towards youth ministry.

The number of churches that have employed a salaried full-time youthworker/pastor continues to grow. A recent survey by the Evangelical Alliance revealed that one in ten of EA-affiliated churches employs a full-time youth worker. Meanwhile a range of organisations such as Oasis Trust and Moorlands College have developed training courses to prepare candidates for the growing list of vacancies.

More resources have also been channelled into new publications. Whereas twenty years ago the number of specialist youth ministry books were few and mainly American in origin, today books and other resources are booming. The launch and growth of *YOUTHWORK* magazine, the inter-denominational magazine for Christian youth workers, from a tentative insert in its sister title *Alpha* magazine into a bi-monthly and then monthly title, proves a rising hunger for youth ministry resources. It also suggests that youth ministry is in some churches taking an important central focus instead of existing on scraps in the margin of church life.

However, it must be said that despite a general rise in the profile of youth ministry, the actual quality of provision varies widely. The gulf between the 'haves' (churches which provide a high-quality youth ministry) and the 'have-nots' (churches where youth ministry is virtually non-existent) is widening.

2. Experimentation

The awareness that past youth ministry strategies have often failed has encouraged creativity to flower. These attempts to make the gospel culturally

relevant have resulted in an experimental atmosphere.

Youth-orientated alternative worship services have sprung up and have gained attention and interest from both inside and outside the church.

The well-documented demise of Sheffield's Nine O'Clock Service attracted huge media attention in the late summer of 1995 – much of it focusing on the damaging allegations of misconduct surrounding its leader Chris Brain. However, subsequent coverage focused on the diverse musical creativity and appeal to young people that the alternative worship scene has.

The difficulty of effectively integrating unchurched converts into mainstream churches resulted in the formation of youth churches (autonomous groups) and youth congregations (a separate identity within the covering and leadership of an existing adult church).

Experimentation has resulted in both successes and failures. But even the failures can serve the useful purpose of helping us to learn from the mistakes made.

I believe the need to seek God-inspired culturally sensitive strategies to reach unchurched young people with the gospel will result in a continuation of pioneering and creative experimentation.

3. Mentoring

Many churches are developing integrated discipling schemes to take young people beyond initial conversion decisions to a more mature faith in Christ. A key component in most of the more successful schemes includes mentoring. Mentoring is a relational process between a mentor, who has knowledge or experience, and their mentoree, to whom that knowledge or experience is transferred.

Most youth workers recognise that although the quality of the programme is important, much more important is the need to provide relationships and friendships which foster faith. Mentoring can take many different forms, from an intense one-on-one discipler style to a more relaxed teacher or sponsor role.

Mentoring is providing a helpful counter-balance to the 'professionalisation' of youth ministry. The danger of more full-time youth workers, more youth ministry resources and better training programmes is that Christian youth work could become nothing more than a skill to be learned and a programme to be executed. It is vital that while we become more professional we do not lose the personal touch.

Mentoring helps to emphasise the fundamental importance of relational youth work. Amid all the changes and extra resources it is vital that we remember it is people not programmes that matter most.

4. Interactive learning

Children and young people are taught at school through a variety of methods. Instead of just 'chalk and talk' style lectures, they are taught through role play, group work, discussion, drama, hypothesising, project-work, problem-solving, interactive computer programs, etc.

Youth workers are learning to use a more interactive approach which involves the young person much more actively in the learning process. Alongside this has come a realisation that people learn in different ways. Books like Marlene LeFever's excellent *Learning Styles* (David C. Cook) are helping Christians to provide

a more balanced programme which appeals to more than just analytic learners who prefer the lecture-style approach.

Youth workers are often in the vanguard of churches who are seeking to provide a more balanced and interactive style of learning.

5. Empowerment

Should we hand over decision-making power in the church to young people? And if so how? These issues are at the heart of empowerment.

Empowerment is about training people to act responsibly with power and then actually handing power over. All too often these two components – training and responsibility – are missing, and this leads to frustration and sometimes rebellion.

Empowerment is an issue which is not going to go away. Church leaders and those with influence in the church need to encourage every member by doing all they can to empower them to reach their full potential in Christ.

Empowerment is a concept which has come of age and is likely to be around for a long time. This is an issue that is much wider than just young people. It affects everyone in the church.

6. New opportunities

While many churches are giving youth work more resources and profile, funding restrictions by national and local government have resulted in sometimes savage cuts in statutory youth work. The numbers of salaried posts in statutory youth clubs has dropped sharply, while some clubs have had to reduce their provision or close altogether. This sad state of affairs presents the church with the opportunity to be involved in the frontline of youth work provision.

However, many churches are failing to seize this opportunity. They continue to prioritise resources towards programmes aimed at churched young people. The reasons are twofold: past failures to integrate unchurched youth and the priorities of those who decide where money will be spent.

Past failures

Attempts to reach out to unchurched youth bring back painful memories of failure to integrate contacts in many churches. Petty vandalism, swearing, aggression and other anti-social behaviour resulted in a decision to close down the club. The young people contacted through the youth club are considered a 'bad lot' and henceforth ignored.

Funding priorities

The people who put the money into the collection plate at church each week will include a significant number of parents. When budgets are allocated they call for the money to be spent on programmes for their children! If the church hires a full-time youth worker the job description will usually demand that he/she spends most time and effort on keeping the young people the church has, rather than in working with unchurched youth.

Detached youth work, working in a statutory youth club and other forms of youth work which are focused on the unchurched are often marginalised, and vital opportunities are lost.

These six key factors – a sense of urgency, experimentation, mentoring, interactive learning, empowerment and new opportunities – make the late 1990s an exciting time to be involved in youth ministry.

It isn't possible to predict accurately whether youth ministry will continue to stay near the top of the agenda. However, with the fast-rising number of full-time salaried church-based youth workers, and the range and number of creative youth ministry projects now in place, it is difficult to imagine all those budgets drastically reduced without some loud and prolonged protest!

What is more many of those currently in full-time youth ministry will, as they grow older, move into general pastor/minister roles in the church. So in twenty years' time we can expect that many of the key church leaders will have formerly been full-time youth workers/pastors. The advantage of that fact is that youth ministry may be regarded by those men and women more favourably than if they had not formerly been in full-time youth ministry.

Youth ministry in the year 2020 is sure to be different in many ways. New technology and social trends will require youth workers to be very creative in their programme planning. But what will hopefully have grown is a commitment to relational youth ministry.

Chapter Two

TEENAGERS TODAY – GENERATION Zzzz?

by John Buckeridge

Surveys of British young people characterise most of them today as conservative, keen to achieve good qualifications, and nervous of the future in general and their job prospects in particular. While Generation X could afford to be radical or rebellious, most teenagers today are too cynical or busy getting good grades to be bothered about much. Some commentators suggest that today's youth can best be tagged Generation Zzzz.

Despite all the negative media coverage of today's teens, which can leave the impression that they all smoke, take Ecstasy every weekend at raves, and are dirty and smelly, the truth is that 70% do not smoke; 80% do not go to discos/raves; and 40% take a bath or shower every day.

Surveys suggest that rather than rebelling against their parents, teenagers respect adults' points of view. More than nine out of ten young people believe parents should have a say in what is taught in schools. And six out of ten believe that sex education for under-twelves should be at the discretion of their parents.

There are exceptions of course. While most teens are disinterested in politics, some are passionate about changing the world. However, these tend to focus on single issues; 'ban live exports' or 'stop the by-pass' is their call to arms.

So what are the factors that have led to what one analyst described as 'the greying of a generation'?

'We're looking at a generation that has grown up with large social change, the disintegration of their home life, fracturing families where Mum lives in one place and Dad lives in another,' says sociologist Tony Newman. 'They have had to grow up quite quickly, and they've seen what's gone wrong with adults. I wouldn't call them boring, but they are certainly more mature.'

Having seen and sometimes been hurt by family breakdowns, high rates of unemployment, ever-more explicit and violent television programmes, films and videos, these adult~teens have grown up fast – too fast.

To add to their worries, fear of crime (82% of young people have been the victims of a crime), over-protective parent(s) and the boom in home entertainments have also eroded their sense of community or civic pride. Membership of most clubs aimed at young people has been in decline for over a decade.

Instead more and more young people stay at home in the evenings or pop round to a friend's house. Youth-dedicated cable TV channels, the growth in the Internet along with ever-more sophisticated computer games systems, plus the arrival of virtual reality headsets mean young people will be increasingly less inclined to leave their homes. When they do, except for the poor, they venture outside in the comfort of their parent's car, with their parents acting as chauffeurs to cocoon them further from real or imagined danger.

Surveys in the United States suggest that heavy television viewing increases passivity and pessimism about human nature. Recent statistics state that 72% of young teens have a television in their room – making parental influence over what they watch negligible. The average daily viewing of thirteen to fifteen-year-olds is 3.56 hours.

However, reading habits have not died, despite the growing influence of television and electronic entertainment in general. A recent survey of 8,000 ten to fourteen-year-olds, designed to replicate one conducted in 1970, indicates that more children and young people read for pleasure than they did twenty-five years ago. The study conducted at Nottingham University found that the average number of books read in the four weeks before the research was 2.5 compared to 2.4 in 1970. It was lowest (at 1.45) among boys aged fourteen – the only category found to be reading less than in 1970.

Magazines are particularly popular with teenage girls. By the summer of 1996 *Sugar* had become the biggest selling title with *Just 17*, *More*, *TV Hits*, and *Mizz* close behind, and together totaling over a million copies.

Julie Capstick, publisher of IPC's *Mizz* and *19*, told *Media Week*: 'Whereas older women regard buying a magazine as a bit of a luxury, for teenagers it is part of their lifestyle – just like buying clothes or going out.' Capstick confirms that girls are maturing much earlier and that the average age of her titles' readers has dropped by up to two years. A Youth TGI/BRMB survey in 1994 showed that the most widely read magazine among eleven to fourteen-year-olds was *Just Seventeen*.

The sexual advice given by the agony columns of these magazines has often attracted criticism. The problem page of February 1996's *Sugar* was typical of many of these magazines. It included items such as how to masturbate your boyfriend and what an orgasm is. In the spring of 1996 a Tory MP tabled a Private Member's Bill to introduce certification controls, like those on cinema films, and to establish a recommended minimum age limit on some teenage magazines. This followed an outcry in November 1995 by parents angry at the explicit advice on oral sex in *TV Hits* magazine. This led to its temporary removal from some supermarket chains. The Bill failed to get the support of the government, who felt the law unworkable.

The best-selling teen titles deliver advertisers with an attractive route to market their products. Huge sums of money are spent on research by the top brands to ensure their ads in magazines and on TV win them a bigger slice of the lucrative teenage market. In fact some of the best research of young people is paid for by advertising agencies.

Their studies show that teenagers are prone to act on advertising messages, although they have a sophisticated taste and reject adverts that too obviously try to be trendy. They also stress the need for regularly changing the ad because teens get annoyed when an ad has appeared too frequently. Surveys show that many ads are not noticed after the third or fourth showing.

Developing cosmetics and toiletries advertising is at the heart of the financial success of teenage girls' titles. Health and beauty clients account for around 37% of advertising in the main titles. However, the biggest advertisers in the teenage girls sector remains sanitary protection and toiletries brands.

Advertisers have a more difficult task in reaching teenage boys in large numbers. Their most favoured read is *The Sun* newspaper followed by *Viz*. This bi-monthly comic is packed with crude and sexist smut, and is supposedly only for sale to adults. Style magazines have failed to attract teenage boys as readers. They prefer computer and football magazines, only graduating to *Sky* and the laddish *Loaded* magazine when they reach sixteen.

Advertisers will continue to chase children and young people because of their growing spending power. According to Youth TGI the 9 million seven to nineteen-year-olds in the UK hold an estimated total disposable income of £8bn. Competition to attract this market is both aggressive and intense, with young people mere pawns in the middle of ever-more sophisticated and cynical attempts to make them want a product enough to buy it, or nag their parents to buy it for them.

Without adopting all the methods of advertisers and big business, there are still lessons to be learned about their methods and creativity. The UK in the late 1990s is a challenging and fast-changing environment for youth ministry. Christian youth work needs to adapt and change constantly if it is to reach anything more than the small minority we currently touch. Identifying different social groups of young people and then providing a culturally relevant ministry to reach them is likely to result in more niche youth work, specifically aimed at a particular group. Some young people are never going to be reached with conventional youth work. An open club, detached work or lunchtime school club will leave the majority untouched. But the scene is far from bleak. New technology provides new opportunities. The number of children and young people who have access to the Internet is growing very fast. Here is a potential window into the bedroom of hundreds of thousands of teenagers in the UK and millions worldwide.

Facts and Figures

Education
* 57% worry about getting a job after their studies.
* 80% think secondary school exam results should be published.
* 82% report bullying at school.
* 69% think that people who repeatedly bring drugs into school should be expelled or
     suspended.

Politics
* 59% have no interest in politics.
* 21% said they supported a political party.
* 45% read a daily newspaper three times a week.

Religion and morality
* 58% believe in God.
* 72% said that if they found a £100 note in the street they would hand it in to the police.

Television
* 86% watch TV seven days a week.
Out of every ten hours' viewing:
* 4 hours are spent watching BBC.
* 4.5 hours are spent watching ITV, Channel 4, GMTV.
* 1.5 hours are spent watching cable or satellite.

Crime
* 77% think reducing poverty is effective in crime prevention.
* 78% feel that greater discipline in schools and families would help to reduce crime.
* 64% feel that a poor person is more likely than a rich person to be found guilty of a crime
     they did not commit.
* 66% support the death penalty.

Race
* 28% admit to some degree of racial prejudice.
* 44% think a black person is more likely than a white person to be found guilty of a crime
     they did not commit.

Family life
* 82% of young women and 78% of young men believe it is fine for people to live together
     without getting married.
* 66% of young women think that one parent can bring up a child as well as two can,
     compared with 45% of young men.

Survey statistics from: Exeter University Schools Health Education Unit, Carrick James Market
Research, Nottingham University, Youth Facts/EMAP, Youth TGI/BMRB International,
YPSA/Barnardos.

Chapter Three

EVALUATION BEFORE ACTION

by John Buckeridge

The little girl ran into the room, squealed with delight at the sight of the bouncy castle and party food and then rushed over to a table where three children were painting. Then to her great delight the party host gave her a new painting book. She stood hopping up and down for a moment in an agony of indecision. Should she take her shoes off and go for a bounce on the castle, or do some painting in her lovely new book?

Deciding on the painting, she ran to the table, sat down and opened the book and then grabbed for a paint brush. But in her frenzied state she accidentally spilled a large cup of water all over her book. Realising it was about to be ruined, she dragged her arm across the sodden pages to sweep the water away. But her feverish attempts to salvage the book only resulted in her getting water and then paint all over her pretty party dress. A moment later her mother noticed her distress and she was led away in floods of tears. In her eagerness to get started, she ruined her present and dress, and had to leave the party to go home and change her clothes.

That little girl is a lot like some youth workers. In their eagerness and excitement to get started, their very first actions lead to premature disaster. If only they had taken a while to evaluate the situation before launching a programme, they could have saved themselves and others unnecessary grief.

If you are new to youth ministry, or if you

intend launching some new initiative for young people, stop for a moment and work through the five principles in this chapter. This exercise may delay you from starting to paint, but it could also prevent the canvas being spoiled!

1. National and local statistics

Find out about the general and local trends that affect young people. The previous chapter will provide a starting point for national statistics, but new research is published all the time, so keep up to date with the latest findings. These will identify information and trends which could affect the shape and style of your youth programme.

Local information about the young people in your area is even more important to know about. Listening to young people is one of the best sources of information. Questionnaires or informal conversations to discover their opinions, values, spending habits, needs, etc, will provide you with a host of important data. Start with the young people in the church, but then go beyond this group to speak to unchurched young people. Find out what they think and want.

Asking the opinion of other key local people such as police officers, ministers, youth officers (church and statutory) will be informative, and will also demonstrate an attitude of humility that will be appreciated. A new youth worker who thinks he/she knows it all and doesn't need any help or advice is not a likeable animal. Don't unnecessarily wind up others who have been working with/for young people, possibly for many years, by breezing in and starting something without referring to them.

Local government counsellors, schools, librarians and the electoral roll are additional sources which may provide useful nuggets of information and advice.

2. Audit the current provision and available resources

Before starting anything it makes sense to find out what existing provision there is for young people. Find out what local youth clubs and groups there are, where and when they meet, how many attend, and what the programme consists of. Then look for the gaps in provision. This process may also show that certain types of youth work are already well provided for in your community. Don't replicate something already in existence when so much else needs to be done. Discovering the extent of local provision may reveal obvious 'gaps' which it might be appropriate for your church to fill.

The next step is to find out what resources already exist that might be available to any youth provision you launch. By 'resources' I mean workers, training,

finance, equipment and specialised people skills.

Check out what is available from your church denominational youth office (if one exists), plus the local borough/county youth service and council funds (discretionary grants are often available). Don't forget the resources of people and finance found in your own church. Ask around and you will be amazed at the amount of money and equipment that you can turn up!

However, a word of warning. Don't accept offers of help, pieces of equipment, or even money at this stage. The audit process is to discover what is around. Not until you develop a mission statement, aims and goals will it become clear if any or all of the help is appropriate.

3. Writing a mission statement

A good mission statement should briefly summarise your aims. It should be specific but at the same time allow room for flexibility.

These aims should be 'owned' by the church leadership and everyone on the youth ministry team, and everyone involved should be constantly working in the light of these aims. This will provide a central focus, especially if the mission statement is written and displayed in a prominent place.

Do not simply try to impose your own vision on other people – they may bale out at the first disappointment. Instead work on the mission statement together in an attitude of prayer, and in the light of the audit of local needs and resources.

I edit *YOUTHWORK* magazine and on the cover of each issue we print our mission statement. It reads: 'Ideas, resources and guidance for youth ministry.' Obviously that is very brief and general, but this succinct statement is at the heart of what the magazine is about.

From this general statement of intent you can then begin to identify the most appropriate youth ministry programme to meet the aims. These options could include:

* Detached youth work
* 'Open' youth club
* Socially orientated programme of special events
* Special focus group (eg football, music, in-line skaters, computers)
* Inquirers' group (eg Just Looking, Youth Alpha course)
* Conventional youth fellowship
* Youth congregation/church
* Alternative worship services
* Peer-led discipleship group
* Joint churches initiative
* School lunch-time clubs/Christian Union
* Assisting in existing church/statutory provision

However, you may feel that no current model exists to meet the mission statement you believe God wants you to aim for. It is important to be creative and open to developing a new style of youth ministry. Having said that, I believe that the best youth ministry always puts the emphasis on people – the quality of relationships; rather than programme – the variety and creativity of what happens.

But the mission statement is not enough. It has to be developed into specific and measurable goals.

For *YOUTHWORK* magazine this means growth in circulation, advertising income, improved evaluation scores on the content of the magazine from our consulting editors who feed back on every issue, and growth in the other resourcing projects we sponsor or organise, such as the Brainstormers youth ministry training conferences.

The ministry of the magazine has goals which, if met, will help achieve the mission statement. These goals are specific and measurable so that at given periods of time it is possible to evaluate how well we are doing in attempting to reach our general aims.

It is the fact that failure is identifiable that frightens some people away from setting clear, measurable goals. But this is a grave

---

What are clear, specific and measurable goals?
Try the simple exercise below. Identify which of these goal statements are specific and measurable, and which are woolly and unspecific.

1. Learn to swim.
2. Read the New Testament within six months starting from tomorrow.
3. Sit on fewer committees.
4. Pass my driving test by the end of this year.

The answer is that 1 and 3 are woolly and unspecific. When are these goals to be achieved by, and how will you judge whether you can swim? Is it a length of the pool, the ability to float, or simply avoid drowning? Goals 2 and 4 by comparison are specific and measurable. If you start reading from Matthew's Gospel tomorrow and reach the end of Revelation within six months, or get the OK from a driving test examiner by 31st December, you have achieved the goal. If you don't, you will have failed.

mistake. Even in failure it is possible to achieve much. You will be more able to identify your mistakes and remedy them than if you drift aimlessly along.

Specific and measurable goals act as a vital spur to prayer and joint action by the team of people working alongside you. It is very easy to get demotivated without goals. When goals are met, there is the joint sense of achievement and source of praise to God which is diluted without such clear targets.

Just in case you think that making plans and setting goals is somehow unbiblical, what about Noah's ark, Solomon's temple or Nehemiah's rebuilding of the walls of Jerusalem? All three required meticulous and methodical planning.

4. Evaluating an ongoing programme

How do you evaluate youth ministry? Do you count up the number of young people who attend the youth club and compare it to last year? Even if the group is growing numerically, how do you balance that against the fact that it is more rowdy, the youth ministry team are getting disgruntled, and destructive cliques have formed among the young people?

Evaluation depends on a variety of factors or criteria. What is more, this is not just some management process – this needs to be a spiritual process. We must be open to what God is doing in and for the group.

So what criteria for evaluation could we use? I'm not going to suggest just one set of criteria, but I can recommend some which you may find helpful. The nature of your programme may require that you devise some additional criteria of your own.

Duffy Robbins, an American youth ministry specialist, identifies two main groups of evaluation criteria:

Event-orientated
eg Sunday night youth fellowship – numbers, programme content, budget (these are easy to quantify, hard facts).

Characteristic-orientated:
eg Spiritual growth, depth of relationship/friendships, levels of violence/anti-social behaviour, commitment to community service/evangelism, relationship/integration with adult church (these are harder to quantify and measure).

Evaluating the ongoing programme by both of these groups of criteria will identify its strengths and weaknesses.

But this process should not be restricted to the leaders/workers. I believe everyone who participates in the programme should be involved in the evaluation process, including the young people themselves, although they may not be evaluating to identical criteria.

The young people may find evaluation forms and questionnaires a more user-friendly option. If these are completed anonymously they may feel more able to be totally honest. These forms should include a scoring basis for each element of the programme, as well as overall. I find that it is best to restrict the scoring scale on forms like these to 1 – 4. That way they cannot opt for a number in the middle (such as 5 on a scale of 1-10). They have to choose one side of the line or the other – 3 being a positive score and 2 a more critical rating.

Multiple choice selection is another user-friendly option for young people who might be less able to put into writing or words how they feel about the youth programme. Statements with a variety of options mean that even the quietest or least co-operative are likely to complete a form.

An example of a multiple choice statement could be:

The tuck bar in our youth club (a) is well-stocked and reasonably priced; (b) doesn't sell the chocolate/crisps/soft drinks I like; (c) is overpriced; (d) is not something I ever use; (e) is reasonable but could be improved with .... (enter comments).

Compare the statements from the young people and look for common threads of opinion. If you identify forms by age and/or gender you may discover that certain elements within the club or group hold common views. Take time and effort on the wording of the forms, and try to avoid any leading questions which might distort the results.

If you ask the young people for their opinions you should arrange a follow-up time when you tell them the overall results of their evaluation, and what ways the programme may change to accommodate the reasonable views they aired. This will validate the fact that you asked for their views. If you regularly ask their opinion and never tell them how their views have affected the structure and content of the youth programme, they will see it for what it probably was – a public relations exercise, with little actual real purpose.

You may find that similar questionnaires work well among the youth ministry team. However, it is important that together you ask these fundamental questions:

* What is going well? Why?
* What is not going well? Why?
* What are the priority problems?
* What are the opportunities?

* Are we reaching our stated goals and in line with our mission statement?
* What new ideas do we have to help us achieve our goals and fulfil our mission statement?
* Is there something we are not doing enough?
* Is there something we are not doing at all but should?
* Is there something we've tried before but stopped?
* Is the church informed and supportive of the youth ministry?
* How integrated with the church is the youth work?
* What current trends are affecting the club/group/young people?
* What are the implications of these trends for our future planning?
* What trends can we anticipate that will have a radical effect on the young people?
* In the light of these future anticipated trends what contingency plans can we make now to be ready for these changes?

Stepping back to evaluate and analyse is a healthy process, but it can appear threatening to more established workers. Be aware of this and seek to put them at their ease. If possible, make a day or weekend away part of the evaluation process. Coming away from the situation, putting some geographical space between you and home, often allows you and the team to evaluate more honestly and accurately. It can also help to put things into perspective. But do not expect this process to be a negative or depressing time! Evaluation means considering the weaknesses and strengths, and time together as a team also allows precious time together with God.

Use this time to review comments made by young people (invite some of them along for part or all of the time). Spend time praying and asking God's Holy Spirit to give you discernment. Ask God to show you what he thinks about the group. Above all, don't organise your time away so tightly to the last minute that there is no space for God to do something surprising. It is helpful to invite a member of the church leadership along to attend to pray, provide spiritual input and be part of the process of evaluation and planning.

A thorough evaluation will provide much stimulus for the programme planning stage and will make your plans much more informed and relevant.

The last four of the 'fundamental questions' listed above are among the most important to ask and consider if your programme planning is to be anticipatory instead of reactionary. What do I mean by that?

I was one of about eighty British Christian leaders who attended an Evangelical Alliance seminar in 1995 where Tom Sine, the respected American Christian author and consultant, said: 'In a world of change we either let things happen to us, react, or we anticipate and prepare for the future. Long-term planning often expects the future to be the same as today. This is a big mistake. We need to be doing "futuring". We need a sense of change. We must forecast before we plan for the future.'

In the light of that statement I believe that everyone involved in youth ministry should regularly be asking: 'What strategies should we be developing so we can prepare for the future?' Even without a special revelation from God about the future, it is possible to analyse current trends and probable future trends affecting young people. Consideration of these means we can anticipate the future and plan accordingly.

I don't pretend to be a futurist guru, but I am going to list a couple of trends which are already present in our society, to get you thinking...

(a) Dysfunctional families

Increasing numbers of children and young people are growing up in troubled homes. Poor parenting, abuse and other negative influences are blighting the lives of an ever-growing number of children and young people. As a result of these factors many are aggressive, have low self-esteem, have poor social skills, and are not achieving their full intellectual capacity at school.

How are churches to develop programmes which will help these young people develop into mature and balanced adults who love God and their neighbour?

(b) Communicating to youth

As we enter the age of virtual reality which includes potentially good (virtual learning) and bad (virtual sex) possibilities, how is the church intending to tap into this new technology and exploit it for good and God?

(c) Revival

Many churches have a heightened expectation of revival. A greater emphasis on praying for revival is commonplace. But if, as many long and hope for, revival does hit the UK in the next few years, the implications for youth ministry are enormous! Anyone who has researched former revivals around the world knows that children and young people usually respond in greater numbers in revivals than any other age group. This is also true of most large-scale missions or crusades. So have we a strategy that can be quickly introduced which will disciple and nurture this large number of young people? Or will they be left to cope with minimal help?

I believe that futuring is much more a statement of faith in God's ability to move, than a clever anticipation of a cultural change in society. If plans are up and ready for the fruit of revival it is a practical demonstration of our faith in God to bring the revival we talk and maybe pray about.

Preparing for the future rather than reacting to trends as or after they happen is a challenge but an important part of evaluating our current state and planning for the future.

5. Building a balanced holistic programme

As young people develop through puberty into adulthood their needs are many and varied. A youth ministry programme should be holistic, treating young people as whole beings. Some church youth programmes focus almost exclusively on the 'spiritual', while others only seem to provide exciting 'social' activities. We need to offer a blend, catering for their spiritual, physical, emotional, intellectual and social needs. Helping a young person to develop social skills, playing a competitive team game, debating a topical issue, meditating on Scripture – I believe all these are of great value and have a crucial place within a holistic programme.

Obviously the size of your group will help determine your programme content. It isn't possible to play five-a-side football if your group only numbers five, while a cosy informal chat is unlikely to happen in a group of twenty-five plus.

Different groups offer different opportunities, and your programme must be modelled around them, not them around your pre-set programme.

Having considered all of the above points it is now possible to consider the specific model of youth ministry that is appropriate, and then explore the programme content, bearing in mind the need for variety.

There are numerous books available with a huge range of programme ideas for youth groups/clubs. If you plan to run a detached programme or some other model, there are virtually no 'ideas' resource books specifically written with you in mind, although you may be able to adapt some of the general programming ideas written for youth groups/clubs.

Chapter Four

STARTING A YOUTH GROUP FROM SCRATCH

by John Allan

So you want to start a youth group? Great. This country needs all the youth groups it can get. There isn't nearly enough serious, committed work being done by Christians among young people.
But before you get started, you should think through six basic questions.

---

1. Has God called me to be a youth leader?

If you ever go to a youth leaders' training event, there is one thing you'll notice straight away. They all look different! There is no one basic type of personality which turns somebody into a successful worker with young people. Good youth workers are not born, they are made – often painfully, after many mistakes!

If you are already interested in youthful pursuits, such as sport, rock music or watching cult TV shows, that helps. If your clothes are fairly trendy, that does no harm. But if not, don't worry. The most important qualifications have nothing to do with your personality or interests. They are:

* A real love for young people.
* The conviction that God has told you to do youth work.

You'll need both these qualifications because they'll be tested to the limit! One of the few experiences I can confidently promise you is that your young people will

occasionally drive you up the wall with frustration and embarrassment! Sometimes the only thing that will keep you going is the driving conviction that God wants you in the job, however inadequate, defeated or scared you may feel.

So be sure in your own mind that you're doing the right thing before you start. Never begin a youth group because it seems like an interesting spare-time hobby, or because the church hasn't got one and the minister thinks you're a likely mug, or because you like the thought of impressing the teenagers.

---

2. What kind of youth work is appropriate?

When they hear the phrase 'youth work', many Christians automatically think of what they know best: the church-based youth fellowship, with a majority of nice, safe kids from Christian homes, meeting once a week for riotous games and once on Sundays for orderly group Bible study. We need such groups – if only we had more – but that's not the only model. You need to work out what your constituency is going to be.

Are you called to work mainly with the children of church families, in the style of Covenanters or CYFA? Or are you aiming to reach unchurched young people – the forgotten 92% of teenagers in Britain today? If it's the unchurched, will it be the biddable kind that Crusaders specialise in forming into groups, or the wilder, more intractable ones that Oxford Youth Works and Frontier Youth Trust are concerned about?

Whichever kind it is, organisations like the ones mentioned above can give a lot of ideas about how to work with the type of teenager you intend to minister to. Study the literature of those organisations, examine their methods, go on the training weekends – and think about affiliating where appropriate. Belonging to a national movement can give you a tremendous feeling of being supported, understood and resourced when times are hard!

The one thing you must not do, in my opinion, is to try to work with too many different kinds of young people. I consider there are five basic groups in most communities:

* Children of Christian families.
* Friends of the Christian families' teenagers.
* Unchurched young people who have a similar moral background.
* Completely unchurched young people who are totally secularised.
* Unchurched young people who are in trouble or at risk.

As a broad rule of thumb, I would argue that any youth work that tries to deal with more than three of these five bands (some would say two) is heading for trouble. You'll be trying to satisfy too many different needs to do more than a superficial job with any one group. Better to determine your aim from the outset.

The one exception to this is rural youth work, where your group may be the only provision for young people for miles around and so may have to incorporate everyone somehow. But in this setting there are often not such wide disparities between young people's lifestyles and outlook as one finds in urban environments.

You also need to consider what age group you are going to work with. If you try to cover everyone from thirteen-year-olds to twenty-nine-year-olds, you won't do it. You will either satisfy one group and alienate another, or end up pleasing nobody. The most natural groupings are usually eleven to fourteens and fifteen to nineteens. Having said that, the youth groups in my church use a different age division. But look carefully at the young people you want to reach, and decide your own age boundaries on that basis.

3. What methods will we use?

If you are dealing mainly with the first three bands of teenagers listed above, you can use a 'closed' approach where young people are welcomed as members on condition that they recognise, and will go along with, the spiritual aims of the club. For others, an 'open' club – where membership implies nothing more than a willingness to come along and use the facilities – will probably be all you can hope for.

Reaching young people for Christ may be your major aim, but youth work has other aims too: developing young people into responsible adults; giving them confidence in their own abilities; stretching them mentally, physically and emotionally by giving them challenges they wouldn't encounter otherwise; modeling for them a mature adult lifestyle.

In the middle of all that, how are you going to declare the gospel? In weekly teaching sessions an hour in length? In a ten-minute epilogue every so often? Or just when the opportunity arises, in casual conversation, after months and months of working to build a personal relationship? The answer may depend on the kind of young people you are working with.

Think through your methods now. You can always change your policy later, if things work out differently from your expectations, but you need to start with some sort of plan.

4. Who is with me in this?

Unless you are an absolutely exceptional character, it will be fatal to try to begin to run a group by yourself. The pressures on youth workers these days are such that you're heading straight for the funny farm unless you have a team of others to help you. Two or more leaders can encourage each other, spark ideas from one another, take more of the strain when someone is exhausted, and combine forces in prayer.

So find someone to help you. And if there really isn't anyone, do two things: first, pray urgently that God will send someone along soon; second, until he does, resign yourself to working with a small number of young people.

Someone once said that numbers are 'the youth worker's virility symbol'. We all tend to feel that unless we have a massive crowd streaming to the youth group/club every week, we have somehow failed. This is simply not true. Small groups have many strengths. You can't have a meaningful

relationship with seventy-five young people at once! If Jesus restricted his in-depth work over three years to just twelve individuals, how many more do you think you can have a significant impact upon?

You also need to consider whether the group will be church-based or interdenominational. Either way, you need at least one church fellowship which is committed to praying regularly and intelligently for what you are doing. Your own church leaders ought to be supporting you with prayer and pastoral advice. Often, sadly, church leaders don't want to know too much about what is happening in their own church's youth group.

Since you are starting from scratch, you may find there is a genuine interest for a while, but as the novelty wears off the attention may drop. Leaders can be so happy that someone has emerged to take the teenage problem off their hands that they cheerfully hand it over to you, never expecting to hear more than the occasional report about a successful houseparty or a sponsored walk. But if teenagers are the church of today as well as 'the church of tomorrow', their development is a matter for the regular concern of the leaders, just as much as the welfare of older people. Be a nuisance. Insist on keeping them informed. Bring your youth group to their attention time and again.

At the very least, you should have an annual meeting with the leadership of your church, in which you are able to review progress together and sort out a budget for the year. Don't be shy about asking them for money. The more your church invests in the youth group, the more it will feel it 'owns' your work. Don't run the group like your private charity; give other Christians the privilege of financial involvement. Working out your budget may be difficult to start with (see chapter 6 on setting a budget), but it will help if you ask the fifth crucial question:

5. What will our strategy be for the next twelve months?

Try to write a description of where you hope to be a year from now, including membership size, regularity and types of activities. Then plan how you are going to get there. That should give you a rough idea of how much it may cost!

'Wait a minute,' you say. 'How do I know what's possible?'

That is where you need to raid the local Christian bookshop and read further on youth ministry. Check out the youth ministry resources detailed in the directory section of this book. You will also find regular help, advice and theology on youth ministry in *YOUTHWORK* magazine.

Do your homework. Later, it may be hard to find the time, and you'll find the research invaluable now.

Carefully answering my first five questions leads to the final steps to getting started.

6. How do I start?

Before the first week you need to prepare yourself, your church, your premises and your promotion.

Prepare yourself
Read some good books, attend one of the training courses or events run by a host of groups from Scripture Union to Brainstormers, discuss your plans with people who are experienced in youth work, and drop in on other local groups to see what they're doing.

Don't despise local authority training for

youth work either, If only more Christians would take it, we would have much better church youth groups.

Prepare your church
Keep them informed at every stage of the process, make clear to them what involvement and support you expect from them, and talk particularly to the parents of any young people you plan to involve in your work.

Prepare your premises
Make sure the rooms you are using are suitable for the purposes you envisage, decorated well enough to attract young people without being over-elaborate, and reasonably vandal-proof. You don't want to spend all your time protecting paintwork or replacing broken tiles. Get your premises right first, and you save a lot of trouble later on. The same goes for equipment you use – sports gear, PA equipment, coffee machines, Bibles....

Prepare your promotion
The best promotion is word of mouth. There is really no substitute for getting hold of a few of the young people and convincing them to try it out. Posters, newspaper adverts, and letters all help, but only to a small degree. Get a nucleus of young people together before you try to launch out, and even if it's only two or three don't be daunted. For weeks and weeks my group consisted solely of three lads, but a year later we had forty on the books.

Starting from scratch checklist

Has God called me?
Do I have a love for young people?
Do I know God wants me to do this?

What kind of youth work should I build?
What kind(s) of young people will I reach?
What age group should I choose?

What methods should I choose?
An open club?
A closed group?
Something in the middle?

Who is with me in this?
Who else should be on the leadership team?
Is my church leadership supporting me?

What will our strategy be this year?
Where do we want to be in twelve months?
How do we get there?

How do I start?
How do I prepare myself?
How do I prepare my church?
How do I prepare the premises and equipment?
How do I prepare the promotion?

Chapter Five

DETACHED YOUTH WORK

by John Buckeridge

What does a church do if it wants to reach out to unchurched young people? Often the answer has been to set up an open youth club. Typically these offer a variation of pool, table tennis, computer games, five-a-side soccer, a coffee/tuck bar and some music. Volunteers from the church staff the club with the initial intention of building up relationships with the unchurched kids who attend.

However, in the past ten years churches and organisations have begun to opt for detached youth work as a creative first step to contacting young people. Since Jesus spent more time teaching outside the synagogue than in, detached youth workers argue that their style of youth work is no trendy new concept! They insist that it makes sense to go where the young people are rather than wait for them to attend a club or event held in the church or home.

For eight of the last eleven years I have been involved in detached youth work meeting young people on street corners, in parks, pub car parks and a stack of other locations where young people congregate.

Not having a building to patrol and protect can be a liberating experience for a hard-pressed youth club leader. But detached youth work requires stickability, dedication and proper management in order to build and develop relationships with what are often the most disaffected and angry young people in the community.

Church support

Before beginning a detached youth work ministry it is vital to get the informed backing of the church leaders. Maybe this goes without saying, but detached youth work brings particular tensions and strains which mean that if the church isn't really backing the work, the project is a non-starter.

Begin by meeting the church leaders to explain your vision. You will need to have done some research on your local area. They will want to know how many young people are around, on what nights, times and locations. They need to be asked whether they actually want these young people in the church – an important question. And you need to discuss together what changes may be necessary in the church structure to facilitate their welcome and integration, when some decide they want to check out the church or become Christians.

All too often work among unchurched youth begins without any discussion or plans for what happens next. If the church is not willing to adopt a tolerant and flexible approach to fostering faith and integrating these young people into the church community, it is better to know at the beginning. Frankly, it is better not to begin a work that cannot be completed. I know of all too many churches which have started to build links with unchurched youth, only to drop projects and programmes once the problems start. The young people are often left with a worse impression of the church than if the church had never begun to work with them.

If the church is committed to the hassle of a long-term commitment to working with unchurched young people then the fun can begin!

A typical evening

As we approach the small group of young people crouching in the shop doorway, a fifteen-year-old announces our arrival to his friends: 'It's the Jesus people.'

After the initial greetings and introductions we sit with them and listen to their news.

'Went to Julie's party on Sunday and got drunk...sold my scooter and got £200 for it...went for an interview at Currys, but I don't reckon I got the job.'

As well as the regulars we are introduced to a new contact who wants to know why we are out on the streets and why we are nicknamed the 'Jesus people'. Before we get the chance to explain, Dave interrupts: 'They come out every week 'cos we don't go to their church, and we call them that 'cos they're Christians. And last week we all went back to Steve's house to watch a video.'

We stay for an hour talking, listening and laughing with them.

By 10pm most of the group have drifted away. 'See you around,' we call out as Dave, Mac and Samantha begin the short walk to the anonymous estate they live on.

Over a coffee back at the church the four street team members debrief and pray before heading home.

Disadvantages of detached youth work

Building a relationship takes time, and there is no short-cut to effective detached youth work. It makes no sense to begin detached work and then stop after three months. It takes that long to begin to get established.

Having made eight weekly visits to one housing estate I well remember one lad, Barry, who asked me: 'Is this the last week you're visiting us?' His expectation of the church was that after a few weeks we would be gone. Only when he was fully satisfied that we intended to continue to visit long term did he start to open up and tell us about himself. It was about three years later that Barry became a Christian.

In those three years he heard the good news about Jesus many times, but it took that long before he felt he had had enough time and information to make a considered decision about Christianity. I'm not suggesting that every unchurched young person will need at least three years before they make a faith decision, as many will need less time. But some will need more!

Detached work is also sometimes very discouraging. Young people are by nature up and down. Their attitudes and feelings change like the direction of the wind. Discouragement should be regarded as an occupational hazard rather than a surprise. Detached work can also lead to a loss of focus. It is easy to lose sight of the aims and goals in a long-term relational work.

For these reasons it is very important that detached youth work happens within a team context. One person on their own will easily get discouraged. Team spirit is crucial, as is adequate prayer back-up. A group of people praying while detached work is in progress reaps dividends.

Advantages of detached youth work

The Jesus-style evangelism of grass-roots contact is what detached work is all about. Making contact and establishing friendships is simple, direct and inexpensive. It takes salt and light out of the Christian ghetto and onto enemy territory. However, it is not hit-and-run evangelism, so non-Christians can observe us close up. The Christian detached youth worker becomes a living Bible to his or her contacts, exposing words, actions and lifestyle to scrutiny. As we show practical love and concern; as we help someone write a job application, pray for physical healing, offer a shoulder to cry on, or go to court with them, we demonstrate God's love in action.

Because you are not tied to a building you are flexible to go to where the young people are. The 'in' places can change quickly, but this is not a problem.

By talking on the streets the young person is under no pressure. You have not invited that person to a church meeting or club where they might feel insecure. On the streets, unlike in a church service, the contact can easily interrupt, ignore, walk away, tell you to leave, argue or question. Because it is neutral territory, they feel relaxed. You have no territory to defend, no church carpet to protect, so you do not have to take on the role of a warden. In fact, you are not an authority figure at all.

If a crowd gathers and the police want you to disperse, you are ordered to move on just like the young people, which identifies you even more closely with them.

First impressions

It was a bitterly cold night and the team had met very few young people. I was paired with Kathryn for the night. She had only just begun working with the detached team and I could sense her disappointment at meeting so few as we walked towards the car park for a debrief. Then, as we walked past a dimly lit alleyway, we saw him.

He was wearing a black leather studded jacket and black jeans, with greasy hair swept back to reveal his large earrings. In one hand hung a large cider bottle, from the other a spliff. He looked and smelled sinister. As I prepared to walk past, Kathryn peeled off and approached the youth. By the time I was standing next to her she had already begun talking.

'Hello, I'm Kathryn and we're from the local church. What's your name?'

His dark eyes focused on her, and scowling he replied, 'I'm Dog!'

Surprised but determined to continue the conversation any way she knew how, Kathryn asked, 'And why are you called Dog?'

'Because I'm an animal,' he grunted in reply.

I attempted to pull Kathryn away. I had seen enough. This guy looked mean and was probably stoned. There was no point in staying.

But Kathryn resisted my urgent body language and ploughed on.

About ten minutes later Dog smiled. When we eventually said, 'goodnight', he waved us an alcoholic farewell and told us he looked forward to meeting us again.

That started an amazing three-year-long friendship with Dog (he had changed his name by deed poll), who turned out to be a gentle and kind man who was attempting to blot out bad memories with drugs and alcohol. Dog had cultivated an image, but actually he was totally different from the hard man that first impressions suggested.

I learned an important lesson that night. Don't rely on first impressions, and don't judge people by the clothes they wear or the company they keep.

Listening relationships

By listening and making yourself vulnerable you can learn. Too often Christians have answered questions that the unchurched stopped asking years ago. As we listen and observe within deepening relationships with unchurched young people, we learn more about their culture, slang, ethics and value system.

As your understanding grows so your evangelism strategy can develop. You can start to consider, pray and work through the issues of today. You will be able to identify concrete terms with which to illustrate the truth of the gospel instead of lazily using outdated abstract terms which mean nothing to your contacts. You will need to translate 'sin', 'repent', 'salvation' and other key elements of doctrine into words, stories and illustrations they understand. You will reinterpret 'God our Father' in the light of what 'father' means to those young people abandoned or abused by their earthly father. Your listening will also gauge the extent of their knowledge and misinformation about God, so that you can start from where they are at.

Actively listening to young people shows respect and kindness – two qualities often in short supply from the adult figures in their lives. Take Sarah for example.

It didn't feel like a miracle when Sarah agreed to my request to get down from the wall. But it was.

The low wall skirted part of the garage forecourt. Dogged by a series of petty thefts, the owner was angry at the kids and he was angry at our church detached youth work team, who he reckoned only encouraged the kids to congregate near his garage.

Aware of his short temper, I was keen to avoid a confrontation like the one earlier that night when he'd threatened several of the kids. So when Sarah, a regular contact, stood on his wall I said, 'Look, I'd really appreciate it if you would get down from the wall please, Sarah.'

She looked me hard in the eyes, hesitated, then stepped down. It was only later I was told that I had witnessed a miracle. 'That was incredible...when you asked Sarah to get down from the wall, she did!' said Marie, my detached youth work colleague. 'I know Sarah. Whenever a man asks her to do anything, she always does the opposite, 'cos she hates men.'

As I talked further with Marie I discovered that sixteen-year-old Sarah had left home after the latest of several beatings by her father. He'd hit her so hard, he'd had to go to casualty for an X-ray on his hand.

I asked Marie why she thought Sarah had responded positively to my request.

'I reckon it was because you had been listening to her and because you asked her nicely instead of ordering her to get down,' replied Marie.

Later, I realised afresh that many young people have few or no adults in their lives who treat them with respect. Not every young person will immediately respond positively to kindness or a listening ear, but it's the least we can do for those we minister to. And for some it may work wonders!

Chapter Six

MONEY MATTERS

by Andy Hickford

Dosh, spondulicks, shekels, readies. Interest rates, budget deficits and price indexes. Whether it is the sound bite of the economist or the jargon of the street, it makes no difference. Money makes the world go round. It causes currencies to fluctuate, markets to crash, shares to fall and heads to spin.

Youth workers today have to get their minds on money. The simple reality is that we can't provide youth ministry without it and yet there never seems to be enough of it!

So what should we do when the ideals of a high calling are confronted by the low expectation of no budget? To put it mildly, it is an uphill task.

A youth budget is in the church's best interest

For too long, too many churches have expected too much from too few youth leaders! One of the expressions of this mindset has been money. Youth workers have even had to resort to paying for youth work out of their own pockets, such has been the church's lack of understanding about the issue.

This kind of no-budget approach has damaged the church. It has stifled vision, frustrated leadership, sold young people short, limited youth leadership to those who can afford to lead and shoved youth work into the murky depths of church priorities. Let's face it what church is going to pray for it if it won't pay for it?

We have to help churches to see that you can't provide quality youth work without money. A youth work budget proves that our commitment to teenagers is more than words. It immediately makes the work that goes on more accountable to the wider church, it encourages creativity, honours the effort and commitment of the youth leaders, and furthermore the discipline of producing the budget creates the helpful environment where aims and objectives are discussed. In short a youth budget is in the church's interest.

A budget is in the youth worker's best interest

Surprising as it may seem though, many youth workers are not pushing for a budget. This often has something to do with personality. Attention to detail is not on many youth leaders' profiles. The very attributes that often make a good youth worker make the thought of sitting down and producing a budget and monitoring expenses about as attractive as chewing on a rat's pancreas! We are into vision, energy and caring for the individual. As long as we can get some money when we really need it, we are happy. It will sort itself out!

This might be convenient for us, but it is not constructive for the young people. It may pander to our personalities, but it will not improve our performance. We might relish the independence it brings, but we need to be accountable to the church. We judge our youth work in terms of the results with young people, yet ironically the way we handle money is a key criterion by which our work is judged by the church leadership. This kind of sloppy approach to finance is a barrier to being taken seriously. A budget is in our best interests. It forces us to be more focused, more disciplined and more accountable.

Budgeting starts at home

Before we take a firm hold of the youth group's financial reins, however, we need to pause for a moment and realise that the problem goes further back. Many of us are not yet ready to deal with a youth work budget, because our personal finances are in a mess.

Most of us are products of credit culture: buy now, pay later. Like our non-Christian peers, many youth workers are equally incapable of deferring their personal gratification. Like the governments of the Western world, we plunder our tomorrow to pay for the wants of today. In the late twentieth century, when it comes to balancing the books, our culture is clearly unbalanced. Before we go to the church leadership with our nicely presented spread sheet we must first put our own house in order. The Bible says that the love of money is a root of all evil (1 Timothy 6:10). The church father, Cyprian, put it like this: 'Their property held them in chains, which shackled their courage and choked their faith, hampered their judgement and throttled their souls.'

In a world of financial chaos, evil monetary priorities, crippling debt and appalling need, the task of any youth leader is surely to model the joy of living simply and sacrificially for the sake of others. How on earth can we hope for our young people to discover the joy of giving unless their youth leaders discover it too? None of us is there yet, but some of us haven't even started the journey. We have to realise our responsibility to model an alternative example to young people. The following maxim is as true for youth leaders as anyone: 'If your outgo exceeds your income, then your upkeep will be your downfall.' We need to rethink our debt and stop the stockpile of possessions if we are to model God's alternative in a material world.

Once this issue is honestly faced, the process of budgeting for youth work can begin.

How to budget

Recruit your team
Don't work out a budget on your own. Draw on your church family for book-keepers, accountants and project planners with the skills to help you come up with the required documentation.

Start early
A year to eighteen months ahead is a good time to start financial planning.

Do your homework
It is first important first of all to discover details of your church's financial track record. Obtain a copy of last year's accounts and get a good feel for general income and expenditure. After all, however exciting your plans might be, there are only limited finances available and your

application will be thrown out if it is not reasonable.

Next, find out what money has been spent specifically on youth work in the past. If that figure is known, it will certainly be a bench mark in the minds of the leadership as to what a youth budget is going to be in the future.

Thirdly, it also helps to have some comparisons. Try and contact youth workers you know working in churches and youth groups of similar sizes and ask them to send you a copy of their budget – it could prove to be a helpful document in negotiation!

Lastly, who decides how money is spent, and what is the process by which that decision is reached? Every church does things differently and it is important that your application fits with the process of your church and that you concentrate your influencing efforts on the real movers and shakers (who, incidentally, are not always who they appear to be, or those who might like to think they are – but that's another story!).

Prepare on your knees

Only God knows the end from the beginning, and the Bible provides plenty of guidance. It is God's future and he wants to lead his people into it, if only we will let him.

Vision is a process. You can't drum up a youth programme with a prophetic edge the night before the budget needs to be set! Vision flows from a walk with God; through consultation with teenagers' parents and church leaders; through prayer and experience. Vision takes time to formulate. We need constantly to ask God: What do you want us to do?

Once there is basic agreement among those directly involved in youth work as to the general nature of the vision, the next

step is simple – start gossiping! Talk to anybody who will listen (especially leaders) about your aspirations, and be open enough to have the vision refined in the process. For the wise, there is a lot to be learned at this stage. Especially draw in the movers and shakers at this point, so that they identify and own what you are up to and will not be surprised by the budget when it comes.

Write your budget

The next stage always takes longer than you want it to! A vision needs to be turned into a time plan and a time plan needs to be costed. Then all the required costs need to be added. It will feel like wading through treacle and will doubtless need to be re-written time and again, but it has to be done and it is precisely here where the make or break of a budget is achieved.

At this point it is important to do your best to research and project for example, taking into account things like inflation and how many young people will be leaving or joining before these figures come into operation. Obviously this is not a science, but it is important to show that you have thought through the issue of a changing future. To help with this uncertainty, try to secure a contingency budget in case numbers increase by more than can be reasonably expected.

Explore fundraising opportunities

Once you have worked out what the vision is going to cost, it is unreasonable to expect the church just to hand over the money. They have to see how the youth department is taking responsibility itself to see the vision fulfilled.

(a) Bob-a-Job – just the job!
People are tired of sponsored events.

Service provision projects are much more likely to do well these days. There is a lot of money to be made through things like: slave days (where teams of young people and youth leaders garden, decorate, clean, shop, child mind, iron, car wash, etc, for a set fee), baby-sitting rotas, car boot sales, etc. We have even held Christmas pantomimes and on one bizarre occasion challenged the local rugby club to a charity rugby match. You would be surprised how many people will pay in expectation of seeing Christians go to the slaughter!

The point is, people are getting something for their money. We just need to be creative. Besides, it helps young people use and develop their gifts and provides a wonderful opportunity for adults and teenagers to work together.

(b) Anything for hire?

Trawl your assets! Perhaps you have a drama or music group that is good enough to be hired on a semi professional basis. Perhaps you have a light or PA rig or video equipment, stage blocks, etc, that can be hired out (NB: don't forget to check your insurance). Advertise it and make some money!

(c) Self-financing

Concerts, youth weekends, etc, should always be budgeted on a self-financing basis. If you can show that young people are paying for their own programme, the church is more likely to put money towards things the young people obviously can't afford.

(d) Grant applications

Applying to local authorities, businesses and charitable trusts is an increasingly detailed and demanding process these days, but still a worthwhile route for securing capital. Just a few carefully thought through applications, however, will convince your church leadership that you are serious about finding alternative financial resources.

(e) Shop around

Always get more than one quote, shop around and borrow a lot! Nothing convinces a church leadership of money well spent more than a miserly youth worker!

Below is a good starting point for a local church youth work budget. The best budgets:

* Are broken down into sections
* Clearly set out
* Give comparable figures
* Provide explanations where necessary
* Are kept short and to the point
* Provide a summary sheet
* Demonstrate efforts to raise alternative funds.

Negotiate

The crunch time in budget applications comes with the nitty-gritty negotiations. The key points to remember at this sensitive time are:

(a) Guard your heart.

Better you don't get what you want than you lose your integrity. Don't over-exaggerate, don't pressurise and don't criticise other avenues of spending. Simply call it as you see it. We are all working to build the kingdom of God after all, not grow the youth group empire!

(b) Justify

Don't ask for anything that cannot be fully justified and be prepared to do just that for every figure – gently of course!

(c) Be positive
Stress the opportunities, if only the resources could be made available.

(d) Decide in advance your priorities
It is unlikely you will get everything you want, so you and your fellow workers must decide what are the non-negotiables and what projects can be deferred.

(e) There is more than one way to skin a cat
Look for angles and trade-offs that will get you where you want to be. For example, if you can show ways of how you are going to make money, you are much more likely to be met half way.

Duffy Robbins, in his book *Youth Ministry Nuts and Bolts*, recounts the story of how one youth worker got his budget rise agreed because he was able to prove that, despite an increase in budget, because the youth group had grown in size it still had less money per head than the previous year!

(f) Rome was not built in a day
Remember that a nicely packaged budget sheet does not in and of itself earn financial trust. Good stewardship over time does that. The best thing you can do for next year's budget negotiation is stick to this year's budget rigorously. Keep good books and be totally beyond reproach in all matters fiscal, and you will be better placed the next year to get what you need. See each year's budget as a foundation for the next.

LOADSADOSH EVANGELICAL CHURCH

BUDGET APPLICATION 1996

This application assumes inflation will stay at its current rate of _____

1. SUNDAY MORNING BIBLE CLASS
- Written Materials ....
- Refreshments ....
- Activities/Resources ....

TOTAL _____

2. YOUTH CLUB
- Decor (details see Appendix 1) ....
- Table tennis table (see enclosed quotes Appendix 2) ....
- Non-alcoholic bar (running costs) ....
- Pool table (see hire terms Appendix 3) ....

TOTAL _____

3. YOUNG PEOPLE'S HOUSE GROUP
- Refreshments ....
- Material ....
- Activities and Resources ....

TOTAL _____

4. YOUTH LEADERSHIP TEAM
- Training Budget ....
- Petrol Allowance ....
- Hospitality Allowance ....

TOTAL _____

5. ADMINISTRATION
- Stamps ....
- Stationery ....
- Telephone ....
- Printing ....

TOTAL _____

6. YOUTH WEEKEND – Self-financing (see separate budget sheet Appendix 4)

7. FUNDRAISING STRATEGY – All figures are reasonable projected estimates

- *Slave Day*   March 97 for youth club
  (50 young people raise £5 each) £250

- *Hiring* PA system
  (10 times approximately in the year at £100 a time) £1000

- Drama Group
  (5 times £50) £250

                                            TOTAL £1500

8. SUMMARY OF YOUTH DEPARTMENT 96-97 BUDGET

Bible class	....
Youth club	....
Young people's house group	....
Youth leadership team	....
Administration	....
Youth weekend	....
Fundraising	....
TOTALS:	_____
PROJECTED INCOME:	_____

The Youth Department would respectfully request £ _____ for September 96-97
      budget.

YOUTH W/E BUDGET
      Estimated costs   £

Programme needs	....
Leadership material needs	....
Recreation supplies	....
Audio-visuals	....
Planning team expenses	....
Venue costs: Basic fee	
Per-person fee ____ at £_____	....
Other	....

Transport: Church minibus   ....
             Coach hire   ....
             Petrol for cars   ....
             Other   ....
Food (if not included in venue charges)   ....
Insurance (if not included in venue charges)   ....
Other   ....

TOTAL ESTIMATED EXPENSES   ....

Expected income

Participants' fees ____ at £_____   ....
Contribution from church   ....
Fundraising event(s)   ....
Other sources: _____   ....
                _____   ....

TOTAL ESTIMATED INCOME   _____

BALANCE   _____

Chapter Seven

HOW TO RUN AN EVANGELISTIC EVENT

by Steve Chalke

With just forty-five minutes to go before the young people arrive, you finally gain access to the hall. You could kick yourself for forgetting to let the caretaker know you were using the church hall for the evangelistic concert. But these things happen, don't they?

The band you booked are angry. OK, they haven't got enough time to set up and do proper sound checks, but musicians are always a bit temperamental. Leave them to it and they'll settle down.

It's only when the guest speaker arrives and asks if he can speak to the counsellors for a couple of minutes that you realise he expects more people to respond to the message than you did. He may have a point about the total lack of female counsellors, but you do have some literature available. What is he expecting anyway? Revival to break out?

At least the youth group turn up, and with quite a few of their friends as well, you notice. Then, as the kids quieten down and the band starts playing, you notice a notoriously violent group of older lads enter the hall. As the first bottle narrowly misses your head it dawns on you: perhaps you could have organised the evening a little better.

Sounds like a nightmare, doesn't it? And yet without the proper planning an evening you had such high hopes for can turn out to be a disaster on legs! Before you start to plan any evangelistic event, however small or grand in scale, there is are several important questions to which you must have clear answers. Many is the evangelistic event that has flopped, leaving its organisers disillusioned, blaming others – and sometimes God – for what was actually failure on their part to think through clearly what they were doing.

So before you rush into planning an evangelistic event, work your way through the following checklist. It will guide you through all the important issues.

1. What is the aim?

The worst mistakes are always the most basic. Before you go any further state the aim of your event clearly and simply in just one phrase or short sentence. It's a good discipline to write down your ideas on a piece of paper. This will force you to root out any woolly thinking.

Clearly defining your goal is important because it acts as a filter as you plan and shape your content.

Sadly there are too many evangelistic

events that try to be evangelistically worship and fellowship orientated, while also aiming to teach and motivate Christians! In other words, if your event is evangelistic, it's probably not the best time to teach your favourite new Vineyard worship song, pray in small groups or take an offering!

2. What is the target age group?

'Everyone' is not an adequate answer. Generally speaking, teenagers will not attend events to which their parents' age group has been invited or are perceived to be welcome at. Neither will older teens turn out to an event they perceive as designed for pre-teens.

Your event will be more successful if its style and publicity are carefully honed to meet the needs of a clearly defined target audience.

3. What is the spiritual status?

Obviously the target group will not be Christians, but what kind of 'not Christians'? For instance is your event targeting the teenagers of church members who have been brought up as part of the church and have sat through endless sermons? Or is it aimed at people in the community who have never been inside a church building before and don't understand the Bible or church etiquette?

Defining the spiritual status of your audience is essential if the content of your event is going to be precisely targeted and therefore relevant.

4. What style and content will be appropriate?

Only at this point are you ready to answer

this question. You may have started with the idea of running a huge concert starring a well-known Christian band, or of inviting your favourite speaker to town.

Now is the time to ask whether, in the light of your goal and defined target group, this is still the appropriate plan!

For instance, if your goal is to reach those who are totally unchurched, the names of almost all Christian bands, DJs and speakers will be completely unknown and therefore have no pulling power.

And just because someone happens to be your favourite speaker, will they communicate with fourteen to sixteens? And what are the budget implications of dragging them halfway across the country for one night?

This isn't an argument against using those with a national profile. You may decide that, though your band or speaker will be unknown to non-Christians, they will assure you of a high quality evening and inspire confidence in Christians to bring along their non-Christian friends.

On the other hand, experience shows that it's just as likely they will cram the venue with Christians who have come from miles around to see their 'heroes' in action. This leaves any non-Christians who attend, and who probably arrive a little later, with poor seats or no seats! What was designed as an evangelistic event ends up as little more than an evening of Christian entertainment. Don't fall into the trap of imagining that the best evangelistic events necessarily have to use visitors from outside. What about using your own local talent?

Should your event have a concert format or a magazine style? Should it be built around a play, a meal, a sporting event, an evening at the local swimming pool...? There are endless options. The essential thing is that its style, format and contents serve your goal as defined earlier.

5. Booking an artist/speaker

If you do decide to book an outside speaker or artist, you then need to go through the following checklist with them. If not, skip the next section.

(a) How do they see their role?

Not every Christian musician or speaker considers themselves to be an evangelist. There are those who see the first purpose of their work as being to encourage and build up Christians rather than working in directly evangelistic situations. The non-evangelist will feel very uncomfortable in a situation where they are required to preach or give an appeal. Many artists will choose to work with an evangelist if they are given the opportunity. Some artists will say that they are not in the business of directly confronting people and appealing to them to become Christians, because their work is primarily art. They consider their work to be a creative expression of the gift God has given them, and only evangelistic in the sense that it reflects their Christian thinking.

(b) What age group do they prefer working with?

Some artists/speakers are better suited to a university or college-type audience. Others are more at home with the local youngsters straight off the council estate.

Check that the artist/speaker is happy with the situation you have planned – and that their style is appropriate to your audience.

(c) Finance

Take your financial responsibilities towards visiting artists/speakers seriously. Even if you are using amateur or part-time artists and speakers you should see that their travelling expenses are fully met at a realistic level – as well as providing them with a gift in recognition of their ministry and its future development. Expenses for meals and other incidentals should also be covered.

If you are employing professional Christian workers it is your responsibility not only to meet all their expenses but also to pay them (generously!). They are often totally dependent on the income they receive for the work they do. Failure to act responsibly in this way can inflict great hardship on them and their families.

Many artists/speakers will advise you about the realistic cost of their work per night or week. If you don't feel you can meet this figure, it is important to talk to them about the situation before they come.

Few artists/speakers will refuse to get involved in a project that is well planned with a clear aim and meeting a genuine need, even if you cannot meet all their costs.

(d) Information

Make sure your visiting artist/speaker has all the information they require about the date, venue, directions, your address and phone number, arrival times, hospitality, exactly what you expect of them, equipment you are supplying and they are bringing, help in setting up, payment of fees and expenses etc.

Having agreed these issues, confirm the relevant information in writing.

(e) Counselling

Check that visiting artists/speakers are comfortable with the counselling/follow-up arrangements for the events and are happy about how they fit into these.

6. The venue

The very nature of some events will dictate where they take place – for example, it is very difficult to hold a swimming event in a church building! But given the option, should your event take place in a church venue or a secular or neutral venue? There are a number of arguments both ways.

On the one side there is the strong argument that we should not expect non-Christians to come onto 'our territory'. It is our job to be vulnerable and meet them on their ground. On the other hand, holding an event on neutral territory such as a local hall creates another problem. People who respond to the gospel have eventually got to overcome the problem of stepping across the threshold of a local church building. If they have already attended an evangelistic event there, then the step is not as difficult.

If you are planning to hire a secular venue, remember to:

(a) Plan well ahead as many concert and community halls are booked as far as one to two years in advance.

(b) Check that the proposed venue is suitable for your event. Check stage size, number of power points, lighting, seating, heating, availability of toilets, kitchen.

(c) Ask the management for a copy of the terms of hire, and read them carefully. You may be required to take out public liability insurance to comply with the regulations.

(d) Make sure you understand exactly how much the hire of the hall will cost and any extra costs for the use of dressing rooms etc.

(e) Check the earliest times you can have access to the building before the event, and by what time you have to vacate it.

(f) Check whether you are allowed to sell refreshments and other goods. In some centres, the right to sell such items is held solely by the management.

(g) Make your official booking in writing. List all your requirements and state how much you believe this will cost. Ask for written confirmation of the booking and these other details, with a statement of the overall hire charge.

7. The date

Any event worth putting on will take a significant amount of time to organise. It has been said that the minimum time you need to organise an evangelistic event held in your own buildings is three months. One held in an independent venue should be planned at least six months ahead.

In my own experience, some of the most valuable projects have taken off at much shorter notice than that, so there are exceptions to the rule. But the general principle holds true. The need for effective detailed planning and strategic thinking is always necessary.

Check your diary, watch out for exams, school holidays, bank holidays, national sporting events, etc. Think through the impact they will have on what you are planning. Also, don't forget to check your dates with your church leaders.

8. Sorting out a budget

As soon as you have decided on what to do and where to do it, prepare a draft budget. This should give you a broad but realistic outline of how you are going to pay for the event you are planning.

Sadly, many Christians have a 'vision' that outweighs their willingness or ability to think through this issue. This leaves them in debt and normally blaming others for the lack of support they received.

To prepare a budget you simply have to balance your income and expenditure. If you don't, you are headed for disaster.

On the expenditure side your budget will include headings such as:

* Hire of venue
* Hire of equipment (ie, PA, lights, video, etc.)
* Publicity
* Administration
* Artist and speakers (ie, expenses, fees and gifts)
* Follow-up material
* Hospitality for visitors (ie, meals, overnight accommodation, refreshments)
* Contingencies

On the income side your budget will include headings such as:

* Ticket and programme sales (see point 9 below).

It is wise to work on 60 – 70% attendance. Never make the mistake of counting on 100% of your seats being taken.

* Sales of refreshments, books, albums/CDs and other merchandise
* Gifts and grants from your church or individuals (including any underwriting you can secure from your youth ministry or church budget)

Don't let your project fail simply because this kind of planning is not done. 'We'll just muddle through and trust God' is an attitude which is dishonouring not only to God, but also to everyone else involved,

especially those who are financially reliant on you.

9. Tickets

Often an entrance fee is charged to give the event 'value'. This fee may not bear any realistic relationship to the overall cost of staging an event which is subsidised through direct giving from other sources. Certain audiences will show far greater respect for an event which has cost them something to get into. Other organisers argue that it is wrong to charge for evangelism. What do you think? Decide your policy.

10. Counselling and follow-up

It is essential to have good counsellors available for the evening and then well-organised follow-up. Many concerts will produce large numbers of converts but if follow-up is not well planned and thought through, most of those who make decisions to follow Christ will be lost.

Often organisers of evangelistic events leave the organising of counselling and follow-up to the last minute. Evangelism without counselling and follow-up is irresponsible as it leaves many people who have been challenged by the event with questions, no clear direction and no support.

Before the event, the counsellors need to meet for quality time together to be clear on the format of the event/concert. In practical terms there need to be cards and plenty of pens (to record names and addresses), literature relevant to teenagers and an invitation to the first follow-up event. People are far more likely to attend a follow-up event if they have been invited off the back of the evening and can take something away with them that same night. The follow-up event should take place the next week.

It is also important not to exclude people who are not quite ready to make a decision but are interested enough to find out more. A regular meeting should be set up in the style of 'Just Looking' groups. They can answer people's questions and look more deeply into issues they may be struggling with. Often, people who take longer to make a decision are more likely to make a stronger, lasting commitment – simply because they have thought things through clearly first.

The important thing is that your follow-up needs to be inclusive, not exclusive. But don't expect these 'new Christians' to fit into the normal church set-up straightaway. Often church life is alien to a new Christian. Look into ways you can overcome this.

11. Building a team

Don't do it all yourself. Build a team from your church or, even better still, your youth group. Divide the responsibilities for the event between them. These will differ depending on the exact nature of your event, but may include positions such as:

* Administrator
* Programme manager
* Prayer co-ordinator
* Publicity co-ordinator/designer
* Press officer
* Counselling team
* Box office manager
* Stewards
* Hosts for overnight hospitality

A real danger with most youth evangelism is that adults end up planning and staging events which their groups never 'own'.

Getting them involved means they will accept ownership of the event, grow in their faith through planning it and be 100% more likely to bring their non-Christian friends along to it.

12. Getting noticed

'Money spent on publicity is money well spent.' True? Well, almost – so long as it's money spent on the right kind of publicity.

Depending on the kind of project you are organising, publicity will be of greater or lesser importance. Obviously, if it is an event to which you are inviting outsiders it is important to spend considerably more time and finance in this area than if you are running an internal event where the best publicity will be word of mouth.

Estimates of the percentage of an overall budget that should be spent on publicity for an outreach event range from 15 to 25%. What is obvious is the importance which should be attached to good quality publicity.

Bad quality publicity is the equivalent of announcing, 'Please don't come to our event.'

13. Prayer power

It's your job to do all you can to organise your event as effectively as possible. That does not mean no relying on the Holy Spirit; it's simply a case of creating an effective vehicle for him to make use of.

Make sure that early in your planning you and your youth group develop a prayer strategy that involves the whole church. All the planning in the world without the Holy Spirit's presence and power will at best simply create a hollow shell. Effective prayer is a vital part of your preparation for evangelism.

Chapter Eight

RAISING YOUR PROFILE

by Danny Brierley

Many youth workers feverishly toil away behind the scenes, like numerous clones of James Bond's mysterious backroom boy 'Q', testing out new-fangled resources on unsuspecting young recruits. And no one is more surprised than themselves when their plans actually work. They are the hidden taskforce of the local church.

Some of the most effective and innovative youth work in Britain is currently being done by churches, some employing paid specialists, but most relying on unpaid volunteers. The tragedy is that many congregations are unaware of just how good their youth ministry is. That's often because much of what goes on takes place outside Sunday services and is, therefore, 'out of sight, out of mind'.

At the same time, under-resourced youth leaders can be ensnared in a maintenance mode, where the 'vision' is to survive the next youth night. All other tasks and responsibilities then slide into second place, making it increasingly difficult to escape from the trap.

To avoid the peril of the immediate takes careful thought and hard work but it can be done. One means of escape is to raise the profile of youth ministry in the local church.

Benefits of profile

1. Prayer

Prayer is vital in Christian youth ministry, for the struggle is not against young people, or those who influence them, but against the 'principalities and powers'.

Without prayer, there can be no success. Youth leaders, already praying for their young people, need to be supported by the regular prayers of their congregation. For that to happen, people need to know there is something that requires prayer, and be given specific needs to pray for. The more profile a youth ministry has, the more prayer will be generated.

2. Recruitment

Finding the right people to serve in youth ministry can be an endless task, yet often the shortage of potential workers in the congregation is not the problem. When Jesus saw the needs of the community, he called the believers first to recognise the need and then to pray. As they interceded, they became the answer to their own prayers (Luke 10:2-3).

People are generally more willing to volunteer for tasks which they perceive to be vibrant and at the centre of God's activity. If that's how youth ministry is perceived, then people will opt to work with young people. However, a church may have a very vibrant and innovative youth ministry, but if it lacks adequate profile then volunteers will be slow to emerge.

3. Finance

People and their churches will give sacrificially for causes they believe in. Youth ministries that are bereft of finance will benefit from increased support if attention is given to the ministry's profile. The months leading up to the church's budget are crucial in ensuring that those who administer and agree the entire church budget have a full appreciation of the need.

4. Young people

Raising the youth group's profile can help promote confidence and 'ownership' by the young members.

Christian young people have a difficult task in living out their faith in an often hostile environment. Being involved in a youth group with a high reputation can make the task of reaching their peers easier. Young people are more likely to invite their friends to something in which they have confidence. That form of empowerment, in turn, can lead to further numerical growth.

5. Parents

Parents often complain that their offspring don't tell them anything. If interested parents are denied access to the youth group, they are left to judge the quality of the youth ministry from the little they observe in the car park before and after the session. However, that may not accurately reflect the quality of youth ministry being provided. Raising the profile of youth ministry among parents will enable them to make more informed assessments of what you are seeking to provide.

6. Youth workers

The average service life expectancy of a youth leader is less than two years. After months of faithful service, many become tired and disillusioned and are 'led' to become house-group leaders.

At the same time, research suggests that the longer a youth leader serves, the more stable and effective the youth ministry becomes.

One way of increasing the longevity of service is to give public acknowledgement to the 'unsung heroes' of youth ministry. Only by giving such recognition will church members be able to appreciate those who work behind the scenes providing transport, preparing the rooms or leading small groups.

7. Church members

Church members need to take pride in the valiant work undertaken, on their behalf, by youth leaders. It boosts the congregation's tolerance and expectation. Churches which have a recognisably successful youth ministry will grow beyond the number of added young people. Families looking to join a church will usually be drawn to those which satisfy the needs of all the family members, so youth ministries with a positive profile can influence the growth of the whole church.

Attitudes

In seeking to raise the profile of youth ministry, it is important for youth leaders to ensure that their attitudes are righteous and just.

1. Added value

The purpose in raising the profile of youth ministry is to enable more young people to be reached and with better resources. The wise leader never forgets that young people are far more important than youth work per se. So it follows that the resources of time and money invested into profile should always remain small in comparison to those invested directly into the lives of young people.

2. Team players

Raising the profile of youth ministry should never be at the expense of other ministries in the church. The aim is not to demote other service areas, but rather to promote work among young people.

Entering into competition with other ministries will only alienate youth ministry and erode goodwill. It is important to maintain a picture of the church being both a body and a family, in which all parts and members are interdependent.

3. Warts and all

Raising the profile of youth ministry should never be driven by a desire for self-advancement. The principal youth leader should not deflect attention away from the youth ministry, with its young people and youth leaders/workers. Profile-raising should also accurately reflect both the strengths and weaknesses of the youth ministry as it currently exists. Failing to admit weaknesses will only communicate a ministry which is without need of help or resources – the exact opposite of what was intended.

4. Submission

Youth workers are called to seek first God's kingdom, not their own. Developing a high-profile youth ministry should not result in perceived empire-building. This will only threaten other church ministries or leaders and therefore not advance the cause of young people.

Strategy

Developing a positive profile will rarely happen by chance, so it is necessary to devise a strategy. It is worth remembering these following broad principles:

1. Nothing ventured, nothing gained

Successfully raising the youth ministry profile takes planning and hard work. Youth leaders, already busy with the day-to-day needs of young people and their programmes, will need to find time to work on the profile.

One solution can be to recruit someone not currently involved in youth work to assist in whatever measures are agreed on. This helps to ensure that those with the gifting and calling to work with young people are free to do what they do best.

The young people should be involved, whenever possible, in devising and implementing ideas.

2. Communicate with the leader(s)

Nothing of lasting value can be achieved without the understanding and active support of the congregation's leadership. So youth leaders/workers need to make every effort to brief, and communicate regularly with, their senior church leader. Any profile-raising conducted in the church will be given added strength with his or her endorsement.

Often a passing reference in a church service or meeting can be very effective, and a little public recognition can be encouraging for hard-pressed volunteers.

3. Money talks

Few churches adequately fund their youth ministry, requiring youth leaders/workers to be frugal in their expenditure. Faced with the challenge of financing youth missions, programme expenses and training, the temptation can be to skimp on quality profile-raising communications.

While not all methods of raising profile cost money, some do, and it is important to remember that whatever you produce communicates a certain standard. Low-quality materials may have a negative effect. The short-term investment of finance will pay dividends in the long term, provided the money has been used wisely.

4. Avoid creating a negative profile

It is important to remember that investments in profile-raising can go down, as well as up, and would-be investors are advised to look for long-term growth.

The key is not profile at any price, but positive profile which communicates value. A poorly devised or ill-timed publicity stunt can create negative, rather than positive, profile.

Youth leaders should ensure that what they do, or produce, is of the highest possible standard, given the resources available to them at the time.

5. Campaign over a period of time

While doing a single activity can be of benefit, it is often more effective to plan a strategy which, over a period of time, incorporates a number of inter-linked measures. For example, at Altrincham Baptist Church, knowing there was to be an emphasis on Christian service, the youth team planned a number of measures to coincide before, during and afterwards, to maximise the youth ministry profile. These included hosting a 'Back to the Future' evening, producing a newsletter, taking two Sunday services and providing an exhibition.

Summary

While the short-term investment of time and money may at first appear to be unproductive, the long-term rewards can be significant.

Successful youth ministry involves a partnership between young people, youth leaders/workers, parents and the rest of the church. Raising the profile of youth ministry can help develop ownership and lead to growth.

An effective profile-raising campaign need not involve high expenditure. Often the best ideas are free.

The communication process is no different from that used with young people.

* First, determine what it is you want to say.
* Second, decide who it is you are seeking to reach.
* Finally, agree on what is needed to communicate the message to the audience.

Ideas should be creative, simple and, where possible, visual.

Chapter Nine

CREATIVE PROGRAMMING IDEAS

by John Buckeridge

Good sources for ideas

* Tabloid newspapers – choose real-life dramas as triggers for discussing topical or ethical themes.
* TV news – video an item from a main news bulletin to encourage prayer or introduce a theme.
* Teenage magazines – a fertile source for discussion starters, talk illustrations and quizzes.
* Lyrics from chart music – apart from the usual love songs, many bands and solo artists cover a range of topics of interest eg, friendship, loyalty, spirituality. Useful for introducing a theme, sparking a discussion, or where appropriate using as a meditation. *Smash Hits* magazine reprints chart music lyrics.
* Agony aunt/uncle columns – to compare their advice with Scripture, or for using in a 'what would you advise?' dilemma, or even a role play.
* Biographies – these are good sources for quotes to use in epilogues or stories.
* Anecdotal/humour books – for jokes, talk illustrations.
* Talk illustration books – there are several books available that contain ready-to-use stories, eg, *Hot Illustrations* by Wayne Rice (Youth Specialties/Zondervan), and *Drive The Point Home* by Graham

Twelftree (Monarch).
* Life/general observation – it's a good idea to keep an ideas file or notebook to jot down ideas, or to file cuttings so that when you need something creative you have a ready-made store.
* TV game shows – I have found many game shows easy to adapt and use in youth clubs, groups, large-scale events. As well as being fun, they can be used to introduce themes such as materialism, greed, disappointment, competitiveness, etc.
* Ideas suggestion box – ask your group to supply ideas/programming suggestions.
* Youth ministry books – the range of ideas books is constantly growing.
* *YOUTHWORK* Magazine – Ok, I know I am biased because I edit this magazine, but this monthly title contains a wide range of ideas, resources and guidance for youth ministry, and is available from Christian bookshops or by direct subscription (see the advert at the end of this book for more details).

A – Z of theme ideas

Here is a list of possible themes for an evening. It should take you a while to exhaust it!

A

Abortion, absolutes, abstinence, abuse, acceptance, accountability, adoption, adultery, adventure, advertisements, advice, affluence, aggression, AIDS, alcohol, ambition, animal rights, angels, anger, anxiety, apathy, apologetics, arguments, athletics, atomic bomb, attitudes, awe of God.

B

Behaviour, belief, belonging, Bible study, bitterness, blame, boasting, boldness, boredom, born again, boyfriends, breaking up, broken homes, broken promises, brothers, Buddhism, building bridges, bullies.

C

Calm, cannabis, capital punishment, celebration, Celtic spirituality, censorship, change, character, cheating, cheerfulness, choices, Christmas, cliques, clothes, commitment, communication, community service, compassion, competition, complacency, compromise, computer games, confidence, conflict, conformity, confrontation, confidence, conflict, conscience, consequences, controversy, co-operation, corruption, couch potatoes, courage, creation, credibility, crime, criticism, cults, cynicism.

D

Dancing, death, deceit, defeat, defiance, demons, depression, desires, devotion, diet, diplomacy, disasters, discipleship, discipline, discouragement, discrimination, divorce, doctrine, doubt, dreams, drugs.

E

Easter, eating disorders, ecology, Ecstasy, elderly, embarrassment, emotions, empathy, emptiness, encouragement, endurance, enthusiasm, environment, equal opportunities, escapism, eternity, ethnic minorities, euthanasia, evangelism, evil, evolution, excellence.

F

Failure, faith, faithfulness, family, famine, fantasy games, fathers, favouritism, fear, feminism, fighting, films, fitting in, flirting, following, foolishness, forgiveness, foundations, fun.

G

Gambling, gangs, GCSEs, gifts, global issues, glory, glue sniffing, goals, God's call, godliness, goodness, gore, gossip, grace, graffiti, grandparents, gratefulness, greed, grief, growing up, grudges, guilt, guns.

H

Handicaps, happiness, hardship, hassles, hate, healing, heaven, heavy metal, hell, helping, heroes, Hinduism, holiness, Hollywood values, Holy Spirit, home, homeless, homework, homosexuality, honesty, hope, hormones, hospitality, humility, hunger, hygiene, hypocrites.

I

Idleness, idols, immigration, immorality, incest, independence, inferiority, initiative, inner city, innocence, Islam.

J

Jesus, joy, joy riding, Judaism, judgement, justice, justification.

K

Killing, kindness, kissing, knowledge.

L

Labels, latchkey kids, late nights, laughter, law, laziness, leadership, learning, lifestyle, listening, loneliness, looks, lordship, losing, love, loyalty, lust, luxury, lying.

M
Manipulation, manners, marriage, masks, masturbation, materialism, maturity, media, miracles, missions, monarchy, money, morality, Mormons, mothers, motivation, moving, murder, music.

N
National health service, nationalism, national lottery, needs, neglect, neutrality, New Age, news, newspapers, non-violence, Northern Ireland peace process, nuclear war, nurturing.

O
Obedience, obstacles, occult, older friends, opinion, opportunities, opposition, optimism, options, order, outcasts, outsiders, overcoming.

P
Pain, parents, parties, patience, patriotism, peace, peer pressure, perfection, performance, persecution, perseverance, personal growth, personality clashes, pessimism, petting, pocket money, politics, popularity, pornography, possessions, possessiveness, potential, poverty, power of God, praise, prayer, pregnancy, prejudice, pride, priorities, privacy, promises of God, prophecy, prostitution, puberty, punishment, purity.

Q
Quality, quarrelling, questions, quests, quiet times.

R
Racism, radio, rap, raves, reality, rebellion, rejection, relationships, reliability, repentance, reputation, resentment, respect, responsibility, rest, resurrection, revival, risk, rock and roll, romance, rules, rumours.

S
Sacrifice, sadness, salvation, sanctuary, Satan, school, scratch cards, Second Coming, secrets, self-esteem, self-hate, self-love, selfishness, sensitivity, servanthood, sex, sexism, sexual abuse, sexual jokes, shoplifting, shyness, sickness, simplicity, sin, single-mindedness, scepticism, smoking, social action, sorrow, spiritual gifts, standards, stealing, step-parents, stereotypes, strength, stress, style, success, suffering, suicide, suspicion, swearing, sympathy.

T
Teachers, teamwork, teasing, telephone, television, temptation, tenderness, terrorism, tests, thought life, time management, tithing, tongue, transition, treasures, trends, trials, triumphs, trust, truth.

U
Unchurched, understanding, unemployment, uniqueness, United Nations, unity, university life, urban life.

V
Values, vandalism, vanity, vegetarians, venereal disease, vengance, vices, video games, video films, violence, virginity, virtue, vision, volunteering, voting, vulgarity, vulnerability.

W
War, weakness, weariness, weekends, weight loss, why, wickedness, winning, wisdom, witnessing, wonder, work, worldview, worry, worship, worth, wounded.

X
X-Files.

Y
Yesterdays, younger brothers, younger sisters.

Z
Zealousness, zest for life, Zionism, zits.

Other programme ideas to get you thinking...

* Themed lock-in (eg, bounce night with inflatables/pogo/super-big balloons)
* Marathon board game session
* Make a video advert of your youth group/club
* Late-night floodlit volleyball/football/hockey
* Hire/borrow a swimming pool – hawaiian party, preach in the pool, baptism
* Visit a cemetery – epitaphs, death/resurrection
* Create a time capsule
* Town/country youth group/church weekend swop
* Decorate a room together
* Dig/clear a garden together
* Parents' open night – hosted by the young people
* Two on two basketball
* Fondue evening – cheese sauce with chunks of French bread or alternatively a chocolate fondue with chunks of Madeira cake, marshmallows and fruit
* Karaoke singalong night
* Christmas in July – celebrate Christmas in the summer around a barbecue with cards, decorations, tree, or hold a Christmas street party
* Junk food crawl – prepare a menu beforehand with prices. Negotiate group booking and get kids to share portions, eg, Hors d'oeuvres: French fries at McDonald's; Entree: Pizza at Pizza Hut; Desert: Apple pie at Kentucky Fried Chicken; Tea, coffee, soft drinks: Joes cafe.
* Hot potato evening – ask vicar/pastor to come and answer/debate hot potato issues and questions from young people. Conclude with baked spuds and beans/chilli
* Grab a Gran – co-ordinate with church/social services for every member of youth group (in pairs) to spend a couple of hours with an elderly person in their home/day centre/residential home to talk, play cards etc. Follow up with an entertainment night where all the old people are invited to an evening presented by the young people.
* Trip to the sea – hire a minibus and take your group for a day out to the sea, mountains, etc. This is especially useful with unchurched contacts who often behave very differently when away from their home territory.

Creative approaches to group bible study

It is important to build trust in a group to encourage them to be open with each other. This also makes praying and worshipping together as a group easier. Get them involved and thinking creatively. Experiment with the use of candles/light, meditation/mood music, guitar/instruments, spoken/written prayers, etc and find out what helps your group to focus on God. Above all, don't isolate or embarrass.

Identify specific prayer requests and regularly pray and ask for progress.

Bible role play
Read a Bible passage, attempting to re-live

the original experience through role play. Allocate each person a character from the story, then as you read the Scripture passage, pause frequently for them to consider how their character feels. Everyone should close their eyes to help them concentrate on their character and how he or she feels as the story unfolds.

Encourage interaction between characters in the feedback.

Location Bible Studies

Make the Bible study come alive by reading and studying stories in their original context – for example, read about Jesus calming the storm (Luke 8), while in a rowing boat on a lake or in a swimming pool, or on a Cross channel ferry, or about God's power to create the stars (Psalm 8) on a midnight ramble during a clear night. This requires forward planning but will make the study memorable.

Buzz groups

Appoint research groups of two to four people to tackle one question each. Each group elects a spokesperson to report back after ten minutes.

Swedish Bible study method

Hand out postcard-sized cards with five symbols in a column on the left hand side. In descending order they should be; arrow pointing up, arrow pointing down, light bulb, question mark, arrow pointing to the right. Having read through the Bible passage individuals should write beside each symbol:

* Something they learn from this passage about God
* Something they learn from this passage about people
* Some new insight, idea or concept they have discovered in this passage
* A question which they have about this passage, or something they don't understand
* An action or deed that this passage compels them to do.

Obviously this study doesn't work on every passage of Scripture, but the gospels and epistles generally work well. This study is good at drawing out shy and quiet people, as they share what they have written. It is also a good thing to keep in reserve for when the visiting speaker doesn't arrive, or some other unforeseen disaster takes place, as it requires very little preparation.

Worksheets

Design your own worksheet with questions or assignments for written answers.

Another variation is to use multiple choice worksheets – check out the Serendipity (Scripture Union) series for examples. Multiple choice means that even the shyest, quietest, most introvert member of the group will have something they can share which requires little initiative or risk-taking on their part.

Rewrite the Bible

Ask your group to put the Bible into their own words. If the passage includes a story, this can be written in a twentieth-century setting. This works well with parables. Encourage them to use modern words and phrases while sticking to the original meaning or message of the passage. The story could be turned into a rap, poem, picture, symbol or newspaper story.

Fill in the blanks

Choose a Bible passage from the epistles that teaches an important Christian doctrine, or choose a Bible study which your group is unlikely to know about. Write the story out on a worksheet, whiteboard or OHP, but leave some blanks. The group attempts to fill in the blanks. Read out their answers, then read out the original Scripture version. Compare the differences and talk about why Jesus or the biblical author chose the words he did.

Chapter Ten

ABOVE REPROACH

by Andy Hickford

Nick was in his first year of teaching when the words of his Head of Department one morning had made him feel sick in the pit of his stomach.

'Nick, I'm sorry, but there has been an allegation made against you,' he said. 'One of the girls from your detention group last night says you tried to kiss her after the others had left. Her parents are coming up this afternoon. There'll have to be an investigation.'

Nick tried to speak. The allegation was so unjust, so unfair. But as he searched for words to defend himself, the horrible truth slowly dawned on him. There had been no one else there. There were no other witnesses to back him up. It was his word against hers. Even if he did manage to convince them he was telling the truth, some mud would inevitably stick. He could see his teaching career shuddering to a halt before it had even started.

As youth leaders we could all do with facing the facts – before a similar incident happens to us.

Fact one: Abuse of young people is common

It's a sad fact of life, but today we live in a culture where the abuse of children and young people is common. Basically, there are four types of abuse:

(a) Physical abuse – where children's bodies are hurt or injured.

(b) Emotional abuse – where children don't receive love and affection, may be frightened by threats and taunts, or are given responsibilities beyond their years.

(c) Sexual abuse – where adults will use children and young people to satisfy sexual desires, (other children and young people can also be abusers).

(d) Neglect – where adults persistently fail to care for children and protect them from danger, leading to serious impairment of the child's health or development.

In 1993, 32,000 children were actually put on the Child Protection Register, but most experts suggest that this is probably only the tip of the iceberg. Sadly we are living in an abuse culture.

In the light of this alarming situation, the government has taken several measures. These include *Safe from Harm* – a code of practice for all those working voluntarily with children and young people.

Drawing together the advice of a team of experts, it put together a series of measures which society can reasonably expect from responsible youth workers. It has, in effect, become the bench mark for good youth work practice today.

Fact Two: Churches have been slow to respond

Unbelievably, many local churches have been slow to respond to the document. Some have flatly ignored it – despite often thorough and helpful advice on how to implement it, published by several denominational headquarters.

There seems to be an absurd notion that such a policy may be necessary at the local youth club, but not in the church. Church leaders seem reluctant to adopt the code because it might imply that current youth leaders can't be trusted. There's even a feeling among some that the church works under a higher authority than the latest 'trendy' government paper.

Not only does that lack of response lead to church youth work being held in disrepute by many, but also such retarded thinking has missed out on something very important indeed. If youth leaders are valued, if youth leaders are trusted, if youth leaders are doing a good job, they need the implementation of the code of practice for their own protection! In our current climate, godly and gifted youth leaders are being exposed to potentially compromising situations, simply because church leaders have never sat down and anticipated some of the worst case scenarios likely when working with adolescents. Such behaviour in today's climate is just downright irresponsible.

Did you know that if a youth leader does not report certain information given to him by teenagers, he could face criminal prosecution? What kind of information, though, and in what circumstances? That's why you need to work through the government's policy document.

Fact Three: The Bible has given us an agenda

I understand that many of us have a natural aversion to the latest politically correct language, the latest fad of the authorities, etc. We don't trust bureaucrats. All youth workers are particularly loath to turn friendship evangelism and relational youth work into a context more akin to a social worker/client relationship. I agree. That would be the kiss of death.

However, what *Safe from Harm* should do is make us evaluate what we do against what the Bible says. We might not take politicians seriously, but as Christians we do have a responsibility to take the word of God very seriously indeed.

The Bible has much to say about children. This chapter is not the place to go into it all in detail, but given our abuse culture, it is interesting to note how the Bible sees the welfare of children as something of a barometer to the state of a nation's spiritual health. When Israel was disobedient to God, children suffered (see Psalm 137:9 and Nahum 3:10), but when it was in a right relationship with him, it was expected that children would prosper (Zechariah 8:5). So much for twentieth-century Britain!

When it comes to youth leaders and *Safe from Harm*, though, the Bible is not quite so direct! What we have to do is take the *principles* of church leadership and apply them to our context. With church leaders Paul is quite clear. They must have a 'good reputation with outsiders' (1 Timothy 3:7) and be 'above reproach' (1 Timothy 3:2). Those two phrases alone are surely enough to convince those sceptical of adopting a *Safe From Harm* policy. It is inconceivable that youth leaders can have a good reputation with outsiders and be above reproach in our communities today without such a policy.

There is another relevant passage. In 2 Corinthians 8 Paul is writing about the giving of money: 'We want to avoid any criticism of the way we administer this liberal gift. For we are taking pains to do what is right, not only in the eyes of the Lord but also in the eyes of men' (vv.20-21).

If the apostle went to those lengths about money, how much more should we when dealing with the lives of children and teenagers?

Finally, when we consider the teaching of Jesus on doing all we can to protect children (Matthew 18:6-10), we don't have any real option, do we?

Fact Four: Church leaders and youth leaders must be alert

I'll never forget a conversation I had in the canteen at one Brainstormers conference. A woman introduced herself as a volunteer youth worker and as a member of her local authority's child protection team. She recounted the story of one of her current cases. A convicted paedophile had manipulated and contrived his way into becoming a youth leader in no fewer than four church youth groups in her town! She asked me to get the following message out: 'All the evidence suggests that determined abusers will work their way into positions of authority with children and young people. To become church youth leaders is an aim for such people. We must be aware.

'When I started in youth ministry I was clear that for me to be alone with a member of the opposite sex was not a good idea. Ten years later, to be alone with any young person is definitely bad practice for any youth worker, irrespective of

gender. That is how fast our culture is moving. It is just not safe any more.'

Let us be clear. Reading this chapter is not a substitute for:

* Working through *Safe From Harm* (or your denomination's equivalent document) with your church leaders
* Agreeing your own church's policy statement
* Initiating the appropriate youth leader training
* Organising appropriate supervision of your youth work.

It is simply designed to begin the process of ensuring that as far as possible the church is seen to be 'beyond reproach' in its work with young people.

Think it through
We adopted a policy statement at my church to:

* Protect children and young people in our church
* Protect our volunteers from false allegation
* Ensure justice for the abused
* Provide appropriate care for all involved
* Be 'beyond reproach' in today's society

Prepare your own church/youth group policy
What's next? The best way to make a start is to purchase one of the following and then work it through with your church leaders.

Safe to Grow, Baptist Union of Great Britain (Tel: 01235 512077)
Safeguarding Children and Young People, Methodist Church (Tel: 0181 444 9845)
Allegations of Abuse – The Church's

Responsibility, EA Guidelines (Tel: 0171 207 2100)
Good Practice, United Reformed Church (Tel: 0171 916 2020)
Church of England Policy on Child Abuse, House of Bishops, (Tel: 0171 222 9011)

Having made absolutely clear the necessity to recognise the importance of this issue in every church's youth work, it is important to say that I do not agree with every detail of the policies as they currently stand. There are one or two times when for me they overstep the line from relational youth worker to professional social worker. Nor do they always account for the different types of young people we work with. For example, my behaviour is going to be different if I am working with a fourteen-year-old girl who is not a Christian and whose parents I don't know, compared with a seventeen-year-old Christian lad whose parents are friends of mine in the church.

Disagreement with detail, however, is no reason to reject the policy in principle. All that needs to happen is that these discrepancies are ironed out in consultation with your church leaders and the amended policy agreement. Then you can prevent a scenario such as the following...

Jenny was as distraught as it is possible to be. Her thirteen-year-old innocence had been shattered by her mother's boyfriend only two evenings before. Now at last in the security of Ann's home, she finally felt safe enough to let go of some of the anger and revulsion she had been holding back. There were no words. It just came out in great waves of sobbing and shaking.

Ann just held her. She'd been Jenny's youth leader for about a year and had 'just known' something was wrong. She asked her husband, Dave, to go and make a cup of tea in the kitchen (in effect to be where he could see but not hear) and she silently prayed, asking God for wisdom.

For a long time, Ann said nothing and simply held Jenny and let her cry. Only when the tea had arrived and Dave had gone again did Jenny slowly begin to calm down. Ann looked Jenny in the eye and said, 'I know something is wrong. I think you've been abused, haven't you? Your mum's new boyfriend is making you do things you don't want to, isn't he?'

The above scenario speaks volumes about Ann's ability as a youth leader. She is obviously a trusted friend, intuitive and discerning when things are wrong. She shows real wisdom in asking her husband to leave the room yet stay around; she is obviously dependent on God, and she shows a genuine love for Jenny. On the face of it, she is a great youth worker, but with one dreadful exception.

With the last question, Ann begins to make suggestions as to what might be going on. At this point any possible prosecution of the offender becomes more unlikely. Ann is well intentioned, gifted and spiritual – but untrained. In this instance it could well mean that the man is free to abuse again.

It is all very well being as innocent as doves (Matthew 10:16), but remember we have to be as wise as serpents too!

Section Two

A DIRECTORY OF YOUTH MINISTRY

FULL-TIME PAID CHURCH-BASED
YOUTH WORKERS/YOUTH PASTORS

Mr John Allan
23 Raleigh Road, Exeter, Devon EX1 1TQ
Tel 01392 411691
Fax 01392 411691
email john@aware.telme.com

Senior Youth Worker
Belmont Chapel (Brethren)
Leads, resources, trains and supports a team of 50-60 workers responsible for the church's work with 3-18-year-olds.

Mr Richard Allen
55 Grinstead Lane, Lancing, West Sussex
BN15 9DT
Tel 01903 755933

Youth Pastor
Lancing Tabernacle Christian Centre (Free Church)
Oversees all church youth ministry. Also involved in schools (clubs, assemblies, lessons), organises evangelistic events and discipleship groups.

Miss Fiona Anderson
Youth Outreach Project
15-17 Shakespeare Street, Maryhill,
Glasgow G20 9PT

Youth & Family Worker
Ruchill Parish Church (Church of Scotland)
Organises a team of volunteers to run school and out-of-school clubs. Regularly visits young people in homes and on streets in an urban parish.

Miss Maxine Bailey
2 Oakfields Avenue, Knebworth,
Hertfordshire SG3 6NP
Tel 01438 813476

Youth Consultant/Detached Youth Worker
St Francis of Assisi (Church of England)
Advises on various youth projects. Trains a team of detached youth workers.

Mr David Baker
7 Plumb Road, Hucknall, Nottingham,
Nottinghamshire NG15 6LE
Tel 0115 9681189

Youth Worker
Watnall Road Baptist Church
Consolidates and develops existing church-based youth work. Works with youth in the community, developing links with other churches, schools, youth work agencies. Training and consultancy.

Mr James Baker
Oulton, Cudworth Lane, Newdigate,
Surrey RH5 5BH
Tel 01306 631054

St Peter's (Church of England)
Leads church youth groups, detached youth club, monthly youth celebrations, leads worship, schools work.

Mr Jeff Ballantine
Southcourt Baptist Church, Penn Road,
Aylesbury, Buckinghamshire HP21 8HN
Tel 01296 26362

Youth Pastor
Southcourt Baptist Church
Pastoral responsibility for children and young people up to age 18, and the staff working with them. Encourages the development of a relevant discipling and social programme.

Mr Ben Bell
St Stephen's Church, 17 Cannonbury
Road, London N1 2DF
Tel 0171 226 7526
Fax 0171 226 7526

Youth Worker
St Stephen's Church (Church of England)
Co-ordinates the youth and children's work, disciples
church young people, does outreach work, mainly
through an open youth club. Visits local infants
school weekly and trains youth workers in several
local churches.

Mr Jonathan Bicknell
210 High Street, Berkhamstead,
Hertfordshire HP4 1AG
Tel 01442 872447
Fax 01442 872446

Parish Youth Worker
Sunnyside (Church of England)

Revd James Booth
11 Hawthorn Avenue, Penarth, South
Glamorgan CF64 3NH
Tel 01222 711374

Assistant Minister/Youth Oversight
Tabernacle Baptist Church
Helps young people to become fully devoted
followers of Christ.

Mr Kevin Braund
42 Mayow Road, Sydenham,
London SE23
Tel 0181 659 8708

Church Leader, Under 21s Assistant Leader
The Barn Youth Church (Ichthus Christian
Fellowship)
Leads a local youth church which involves
discipleship, evangelism, schools work, and
community action. Also oversees the work among
under 21s throughout Ichthus, which involves
pastoring those who lead on the ground.

Mr Danny Brierley
Altrincham Baptist Church, Hale Road,
Altrincham, Cheshire WA14 2EW
Tel 0161 941 2018
Fax 0161 941 2064

Youth & Children's Director
Altrincham Baptist Church
Develops and directs the church's youth and
children's ministry. Member of the pastoral team.
Emphasis on training and equipping volunteers.
External training undertaken if of benefit to North-
West England.

Mr Graham Bright
Flat 2, 120 Station Road, Knowle,
Solihull, West Midlands B93 0HJ
Tel 01564 770528

Youth Worker
Arden Church (Charismatic)
Reaches and disciples young people (11-16) through
work in two local schools. Also involved in an
ecumenical nightclub and coffee bar project.

Mr Peter Brooks
Church of Christ the King,
21/23 Clarendon Villas, Hove ,
Sussex BN3 3RE
Tel 01273 747687
Fax 01273 889394

Youth Pastor/Elder/Evangelist
Church of Christ the King (New Church - New
Frontiers)
Oversees 15-19s ministry in the church, involving
discipleship of both youth leaders and young people.
Also reaches out evangelistically to Brighton/Hove
area.

Mr Darren Brown
102-104 Brettell Lane, Amblecote,
Stourbridge, West Midlands DY8 4BS
Tel 01384 370365
Fax 01384 444514

Youth Director
Amblecote Christian Centre (Pentecostal)
Oversees a youth outreach club, a 10-13s group, and a 14-plus group. Also responsible for schools ministry, special events and a Sunday evening alternative youth service.

Mr & Mrs Matt & Gemma Brown
Barnsbury Youth Project, All Saints
Church, Carnegie Street, Islington,
London N1 9QW
Tel 0171 837 0720

Youth Project Leaders
Barnsbury Team Ministry (Church of England)
Leads the local church in evangelism and discipleship among 11-20s, especially through small peer groups (A-Teams), schools work, detached work, Bible study, prayer, summer camps and football ministry.

Alison Browning
62 Fisher Road, Newton Abbot, Devon
TQ12 2NB
Tel 01626 335242
Fax 01626 331856

Pastor
Vineyard House Church (Independent)
Oversees youth church, evangelistic training and church planting as part of 'River of Life' ministries.

Mr Ian Burton
22 Southgate Drive, Towcester, Northants
NN12 6JQ
Tel 01327 358214

Youth Pastor
Towcester Baptist Church
Oversees all areas of youth work. Plans to expand into schools and community work in the future.

Mr Paul Carter
Plymouth Methodist Central Hall, Eastlake
Street, Plymouth, Devon PL1 1BA
Tel 01752 660997
Fax 01752 229911

Youth Worker
Methodist Central Hall
Facilitates and oversees children's and youth work at the church for those between 8 and 18, and works with other youth organisations. Also seconded to the YMCA to organise lunchtime groups and youth clubs.

Mr Steve Christian
Whetstone Baptist Church, King Street,
Whetstone, Leicester LE8 6LS
Tel 0116 247 7218

Assistant Minister with special responsibility for youth work.
Whetstone Baptist Church
Oversees and trains the church in its work with the young people as well as providing and facilitating their pastoral care. Develops new initiatives, and is involved in local school lessons and assemblies.

Mr Anthony Clowes
40 Garnett Avenue, Kirkdale, Liverpool,
Merseyside L4 1TS
Tel 0151 944 1952

Youth Evangelist
St Lawrence Church (Church of England)
Assemblies, lessons and Christian Unions in schools. Leads a monthly youth church meeting, preaches and teaches in a local prison, college and university. Also leads worship and is involved in musical performances.

Mr Jeremy Coles
10 Carr House Lane, Wyke, Bradford,
West Yorkshire BD12 8DD
Tel 01274 677699

Young People's Worker
Wyke Christian Fellowship (Independent)
A deacon and worship leader responsible for the youth and children's programme (5-18s). This includes four mid-week clubs, oversses the Junior Fellowship and regular assemblies and RE lessons in ten local schools.

Mr Bernard Comissiong
Christ Church, Northcourt Road,
Abingdon, Oxfordshire ON14 1PN
Tel 01235 522549

Youth Worker
Christ Church (Church of England)
Develops and maintains youth work (11+) in the church, building up relationships with pupils in a local school. Also trains and supports voluntary youth workers.

Mr Martin Cornes
St Peter's House, 22 Rectory Road,
Farnborough, Hampshire GU14 7BY
Tel 01252 513377
Fax 01252 513377
email 101521.524@compuserve.com

Youth Worker
St Peter's (Church of England)
Oversees all youth and children's work (0-25). Also serves on a leadership team for evening 'youth friendly' services, as well as being part of a general church staff team.

Revd Geoff Cook
Emmanuel Baptist Church, 55 Windmill Street, Gravesend, Kent DA12 1BA
Tel 01474 568498

Associate Minister
Emmanuel Baptist Church
Oversees voluntary workers in three congregations which offer Sunday and midweek children's activity groups, youth house groups, open youth club and school assemblies.

Mr & Mrs Tony & Sandra Crawford
Heywood Baptist Church, Rochdale Road,
Heywood, Lancashire OL10 1LG
Tel 01706 366162

Associate Pastors with special responsibility for youth
Heywood Baptist Church
They establish, maintain and develop a work among children and young people (0-25), both within the church youth programme and through outreach in schools and secular youth centres.

Mr Tim Crook
41 Lambhay Hill, The Barbican, Plymouth,
Devon PL1 2NW
Tel 01752 664655

Youth Worker
St Andrew's (Church of England)
Leads 'Fish Shop', a 14-18s youth programme, and works as pastor-teacher and evangelist among young people in the church and the city of Plymouth.

Ms Carole Dick
16 Menstrie Road, Tullibody, Alloa
FK10 2RG
Tel 01259 213236
Fax 01259 213236

Presbytery Youth and Young Adult Adviser
Stirling Presbytery (Church of Scotland)
Promotes outreach and worship relevant to young people. Encourages churches to examine their openness to young people. Oversees existing youth groups and trains their leaders.

Mr Gareth Dickinson

Christ Church Office, Christchurch Road,
Winchester, Hampshire SO23 9SR
Tel 01962 864643

Youth Minister
Christ Church (Church of England)
Has overall pastoral care for all church groups for 11-25s and oversight of youth congregation 'Sound Wave'. Also assemblies and lessons in local schools.

Miss Adrienne Donaldson

Cults West Church, Quarry Road, Cults,
Aberdeen AB1 9ET
Tel 01224 869566

Youth Worker
Cults West Parish (Church of Scotland)
Identifies, develops and implements opportunities to increase the involvement of young people in the church. Develops Christian understanding and values in the young people. Also strengthens existing organisations and provides advice and support to leaders.

Mr Simon Douglas

146 Bromwich Road, Worcester WR2 4AS
Tel 01905 424852

Pastor
Bromwich Road Mission (Interdenominational)
Oversight of Open Youth Club, informal discussion group and discipleship group. Works with secular agencies and develops ecumenical youth work in West Worcester.

Mrs Linda Dunnett

44 Forfar Avenue, Glasgow G52 3JQ
Tel 0141 883 5956

Outreach Worker
Orchardhill Parish Church (Church of Scotland)
Trains youth leaders and potential leaders in reaching and keeping 11-19s. Nurtures 20-35s using Alpha courses, parents and toddlers and special interest groups. Initiates new forms of worship and outreach. Also national training of youth leaders.

Mr Jonathan Dyson

10 Prince Charles Close, Penrith, Cumbria
CA11 8JD
Tel 01768 891723
Fax 01768 891723

Rural Young Adults Worker
Penrith Methodist Church
Identifies and meets the needs of young adults living in isolated rural areas. Provides information and resources to young people while giving a positive image of the church.

Mr Dave Eadie

1 Sheldon Court, High Street, Cheam,
Surrey SM3 8RJ
Tel 0181 288 0732
Fax 0181 288 0733

Youth and Schools Worker
Cheam Community Church (New Church)
Responsible for work in secondary schools across the borough of Sutton, oversees church youth work and organises evangelism with other churches in two borough-wide youth projects.

Revd Jon Eastwood

6 Narcot Way, Chalfont St Giles,
Buckinghamshire HP8 4DW

Youth Director
Gold Hill Baptist Church
Directs the children's and youth ministry, develops schools work, discipleship programmes for 11+, directs summer missions, young people's Alpha courses and 'Rock the Flock' Christian music concerts.

Mr Jonathan Edwards
18 Priors Walk, Newport, Isle of Wight
PO30 5RW

Youth Pastor
Castlehold Baptist Church
Oversees the children's and youth work within the
church, with particular responsibility for non-
uniformed youth work, the pastoral care of teenagers
and the equipping and training of youth workers.

Mr Simon Elliott
Brickhill Baptist Church, Brickhill Drive,
Bedford MK41 7QZ
Tel 01234 273773
Fax 01234 273774

Full-time Youth Leader
Brickhill Baptist Church
Overall responsibility for work among 11-18s. Also
involved in schools work, a non-alcoholic bar and a
discipleship programme.

Ms Heidi Ellison
St Luke's Church Centre, 201 Front Lane,
Cranham, Upminster, Essex RM14 1LD
Tel 01708 222562
Fax 01708 223253

Youth Minister
*Cranham Park Fellowship [St Luke's] (Church of
England)*
Oversees the youth work (11-19s) with particular
emphasis on evangelism, training, encouraging and
developing other youth leaders. Also disciples and
has pastoral oversight of the young people within the
fellowship.

Mr Dominic Farango
Crusader House Flat, 118 Upper Shirley
Avenue, Southampton, Hampshire
SO15 5NN
Tel 01703 398521

Youth Worker
St James (Church of England)
Oversees the young people's ministry for a parish
church with five congregations.

Mr David Fenton
4 Canterbury Avenue, Sheffield S10 3RT
Tel 0114 230 1928
Fax 0114 230 6568

Youth and Children's Co-ordinator
Christ Church Fulwood (Church of England)
Primarily works at developing an integrated children's
and youth teaching programme. Also adapts 'youth
methods' to 7-11s and is developing a training
programme.

Sister Val Fernandez
146 Mount Hill Road, Kingswood, Bristol
BS15 2SX
Tel 0117 967 1384

Youth and Community Worker
Holy Trinity and Ascension (Church of England)
Co-ordinates all children's and youth work, including
school assemblies and bridge-building with
uniformed organisations. Also developing ecumenical
youth work under 'Churches Together' umbrella.

Mr Stephen Fishbacher
The Flat, 10 Broughton Street, Edinburgh
EH1 3RH
Tel 0131 556 6212
Fax 0131 556 0492

Youth Worker
St Paul's & St George's Church (Scottish Episcopal)
Oversees and co-ordinates youth and children's work
in the church and local community. Also develops
children's projects in the Edinburgh area.

Mr Simon Ford
50 Willowdene Close, Ashley, New Milton, Hampshire BH25 5BX
Tel 01425 622360

Pastor for Youth and Evangelism
Ashley Baptist Church
Co-ordinates and develops the church's work in reaching and keeping children and young people. Recruits and trains new leaders and involved in local schools. Also co-ordinates the church evangelistic programme.

Mr Andie Frost
292 Croyland Road, Edmonton, London N9 7BG
Tel 0181 807 6032

Youth Worker
Croyland Evangelical Church (Ichthus-linked)
Oversees children's and youth work (3-25s) and supervises a team of voluntary workers.

Mr Andrew Gardiner
4 Bainbridge Avenue, Hartley, Plymouth, Devon PL3 5QZ
Tel 01752 791993/01752 228094

Youth Director
Mutley Baptist Church
Directs and co-ordinates the work among children, teenagers and 20s. Runs youth clubs, football outreach, school assemblies, and trains church members into outreach among young people. Also prepares young people for responsible leadership.

Mr Paul Gibbs
234 Kenyon Lane, Moston, Manchester M40 5EH
Tel 0161 683 5100

Youth Pastor
Sharon Church (Pentecostal)
Oversees and trains schools and youth workers in UK and abroad, speaking at events, advising churches regarding schools work strategy and youth evangelism.

Mr Nav Gillon
Emmanuel Baptist Church, 55 Windmill Street, Gravesend, Kent DA12 1BA
Tel 01474 568498

Student Youth Minister
Emmanuel Baptist Church
Oversees open youth club, multi-media presentations, teaching Sunday morning youth group, visiting teenagers and discipling in one-to-one relationships.

Miss Melanie Glass
Bracknell Family Church, Church Road, Bracknell, Berkshire RG12 1EH
Tel 01344 862699
Fax 01344 304154

Bracknell Family Church (New Frontiers)
Responsible for the 11-18s youth work within the church and, through the work undertaken, reaches those outside the church. Currently provides Bible groups, youth groups, club nights, discipling and commitment courses.

Mr Tim Grose
Leyland Baptist Church, 247 Leyland Lane, Leyland, Preston, Lancashire PR5 3HL
Tel 01772 623603

Youth & Community Worker
Spurgeon's Child Care/Leyland Baptist Church
Works with young people and families in the local community which involves running a Family Centre, schools work and a homeless project.

Mr Simon Hall
204 King Lane, Leeds LS17 6AA
Tel 0113 269 3742
Fax 0113 269 0722

Youth Pastor
Sharing Life (Baptist Church Network)
Oversees and trains a team working with 11-25s,
school- and centre-based evangelism and a youth
congregation. Trains and writes about youth ministry;
also writes songs.

Mr Malcolm Halliday
Queen's Road Baptist Church,
Queen's Road,
Coventry CV1 3EG

Youth Pastor
Queen's Road, Coventry (Baptist)
Supports and develops children's and youth work.
Responsible for a schools-based kids club. Religious
producer for Independent Local Radio. Also produces
youth study materials for inter-church pub-based
youth event.

Mr Duncan Hanton
Queen's Road Church, 30 Queen's Road,
Wimbledon, London SW19 8LR
Tel 0181 947 1859
Fax 0181 947 8995
email 101560.463@compuserve.com

Youth Pastor
Queen's Road Church (New Frontiers)
Oversees the development, discipleship and
outreach for 11s to student age through monthly
youth service, small groups, two open clubs and two
football teams. Also oversees New Frontiers
International youth work for London.

Mr Robert Hare
17 The Albion, Main Road, Edenbridge,
Kent TN8 6HR
Tel 01732 864401

Youth Minister
Edenbridge Baptist Church
Reaches and communicates faith to 11-18s and
encourages them to live out their faith within
mainstream church life.

Mr Geoff Harley-Mason
Youth Office, St Lawrence House,
1717 High Street, Knowle, Solihull,
West Midlands B93 0LN
Tel 01564 778802
Fax 01564 779123

Youth Worker
Knowle Parish Church (Church of England)
Overall responsibility for work with 11-18s, secondary
school work, and the leadership and training of
church youth teams.

Mr James Harpur
6 Church Street, Kempsey,
Worcester WR5 3JG
Tel 01905 820084

Youth Leader/Evangelist
Kempsey Baptist Church (Baptist/New Frontiers)
Oversees children's and youth work, with particular
emphasis on evangelism and discipleship. Also
oversees Jesus in the City, an inter-church youth
work.

Mr John Hawksworth
21 Stannington Avenue, Heaton,
Newcastle-upon-Tyne NE6 5AA
Tel 0191 265 8081

Director of Youth Ministry
Heaton Baptist Church
Directs and trains the church in reaching and
discipling 0-19s. Also involved in three secondary
school lunchtime groups, community youth work and
oversight of student ministry.

Mr David Hibbin
Frinton Free Church, Connaught Avenue,
Frinton-on-Sea, Essex CO13 9PN
Tel 01255 679585
Fax 01255 676511

Youth Minister
Frinton Free Church (Baptist)
Pastoral care and leadership of youth and children's team members, plus young people in and associated with the church aged 5-25. Also part-time RE teacher and sports coach at local school.

Miss Sarah Hillman
Manor Farm, Hill Road, Marcham,
Abingdon, Oxfordshire OX13 6NZ
Tel 01865 391097

Youth Worker/Pastoral Assistant
All Saints', Marcham with Garford (Church of England)
Co-ordinates youth and children's work in the church, including the leadership of a Sunday morning group and three midweek groups. Also schools work and building links with unchurched, particularly through a drop-in coffee bar.

Mr Andrew Hills
104 Hopton Road, Stevenage,
Hertfordshire SG1 2LG
Tel 01438 361798

Assistant Pastor
Bunyan Baptist Church
Oversees older teens work, discipleship class, 15-plus group, alcohol-free bar. Is forming and implementing 'Safe to Grow' policy. Social action issues and friendship evangelism. Also linking inter-denominational youth work in North Hertfordshire.

Mr David Hitchcock
Tonbridge Baptist Church,
Darenth Avenue, Tonbridge, Kent
TN10 3HZ
Tel 01732 352824
Fax 01732 369453

Youth Minister
Tonbridge Baptist Church
Oversees and trains the church in reaching and keeping 5-25s, with special responsibility for 11-18s. Facilitates ecumenical youth work and chaplaincy at a local comprehensive school.

Miss Diane Holmes
23 Raymond Road, Shirley,
Southampton, Hampshire SO15 5AG
Tel 01703 496424

Youth Worker
St James' (Church of England)
Oversees the youth ministry for a parish church with five congregations.

Mr Matthew Hughes
5 Girtin Close, Bedworth, Nuneaton,
Warwickshire CV12 8UA
Tel 01203 491235/317835
Fax 01203 643503

Youth Minister
Bedworth Christian Centre (Assembly of God)
Oversees a team of leaders who develop and create projects for the children and youth of Bedworth. Responsible for a youth club, youth group, children's club, Sunday school and a double-decker bus outreach.

Mr Andy Humm
Pinner United Reformed Church,
Paines Lane, Pinner, Middlesex HA5 3BL
Tel 0181 429 3819

Youth Worker
Pinner Association of Churches (Ecumenical)
Supports and works alongside the youth work programmes already established, and is developing new areas of youth work both inside and outside the churches. Also creating links with uniformed organisations and schools in the community.

Mr Tudor Humphries
Kingswell Centre, Arthur Street,
Oswestry, Shropshire SY11 1JN
Tel 01691 655126
Fax 01691 654064

Centre Manager/Senior Worker
Kingswell Centre/Spurgeon's Child Care (FIEC affiliated)
Open youth work in three clubs with 9-18s, helps provide alternatives to custody for young adults in partnership with the Probation Service. Preventative work with young people and their families in partnership with Social Services. Also neighbourhood work with the church on a poorly serviced local estate.

Mr Edward Ibberson
Wadsley Grove, Worrall Road,
Sheffield S6 4BE
Tel 0114 234 3955

Youth Worker
Leigh Road Baptist Church
Church-based work with age 10-plus, including youth groups, non-alcoholic youth bar and schools work. Also trains young people in discipleship and evangelism.

Mr Chris Jarvis
Church of Christ the King, Clarendon
Villas, Hove, Sussex, BN3 3RE
Tel 01273 747687
Fax 01273 889394

Children's & Youth Pastor
Church of Christ the King (New Frontiers)
Oversees children's and youth work (0-15s), also schools work.

Mr Andy & Mrs Chris Jeffrey
5 Cherry Gardens, Broadstairs,
Kent CT10 2NE
Tel 01843 867039

Youth Co-ordinators
Beaconsfield House Christian Fellowship (Evangelical Free Church)
Co-ordinate and oversee the teaching and activities of 5-18s. Co-pastoral care of leaders, helpers and families of all age groups.

Mr Ed Jeffrey
9 Millmead Terrace, Guildford,
Surrey GU2 5AT

Youth Pastor
Guildford Baptist Church
Oversees the work of discipling 11-21s, ongoing training of current and new youth leaders, teaching and pastoring, as well as helping oversee a townwide cross-church initiative to reach Christian and non-Christian youth.

Mr Keith Jewell
Lansdowne Baptist Church,
7-9 Lansdowne Road, Bournemouth,
Dorset BH1 1SB
Tel 01202 297977
Fax 01202 317054

Youth Director
Lansdowne Baptist Church
Oversees the church's work with 11-30s, split into three distinct groups. Is developing links with local schools and the local university.

Mr Mark Jolly
Kings Centre, 673 Galvin Road, Slough,
Berkshire SL1 4QN
Tel 01753 533411
Fax 01753 539683

King's Church
Oversees schools work team, youth groups and youth-oriented events.

Mr Pete Kelsall
Aldridge Methodist Church, Anchor Road,
Aldridge, Walsall, West Midlands
WS9 8PT
Tel 01922 59875

Youth/Schools Worker
Aldridge Methodist Church
Develops and promotes church-based open youth
work, weekly input to Year 10/11 RE/PSE lessons,
Christian Union group and assemblies.

Mr Billy Kennedy
Central Hall, St Mary Street,
Southampton, Hampshire SO14 1NF
Tel 01703 237700
Fax 01703 234555

Youth & Student Work Director
Community Church (New Church)
Responsible for all youth and student work, including
training of youth and student workers, development
of a youth congregation and outreach programme.

Mr Jim Kilpin
24 Court Road, Balsall Heath,
Birmingham B12 9LQ
Tel 0121 440 0924
Fax 0121 766 7803

Youth Minister
Small Heath Baptist Church
Attracts, trains and releases young people into the
kingdom of God through schools work, detached
work and church-based work in a multi-ethnic
environment.

Mr Andrew Le Roux
3 Streamside, Albany Road, Fleet,
Hampshire GU13 9PH
Tel 01256 702821
Fax 01256 702821

Youth Worker & Evangelist
The Vine Church (New Frontiers)
Oversees and develops ministry to 7-18s within two
churches and their communities. Responsible for four
church clubs, two school clubs and school
assemblies. Also oversees a regional youth initiative
involving eleven Hampshire churches.

Revd Nick Lear
134 New Street, Horsham, West Sussex
RH13 5EE
Tel 01403 240646

Youth Minister
Brighton Road Baptist Church
Oversees the youth and children's work in the
church; trains and encourages group leaders, visits
local schools for assemblies and pastors the young
people.

Mr Jay Lennartson
14 Roland Crescent, Glasgow G77 5JT
Tel 0141 616 0798
Fax 0141 616 0798

Youth Minister
Maxwell Mearns Castle Church (Church of Scotland)
Co-ordinates activities, teaching, vision and direction
in the church as it applies to young people of
secondary school age to early 20s. This includes
resourcing and supporting those who are working
with the young people.

Mr David Llewelyn
31 Chantry Close, Teignmouth, Devon
TQ14 8FE
Tel 01626 773000

Associate Minister
Teignmouth Baptist Church
Responsible for all youth and children's work within
the church; including oversight of youth and
children's workers. Hands-on responsibility for 11-18s
groups and schools programme.

Mr Ian Long
Trinity Cottage, 3 Old Hospital Lane,
Tewkesbury, Gloucestershire GL20 5NQ
Tel 01684 274259

Youth/Pastoral Assistant
Holy Trinity (Church of England)
Co-ordinates under 25s work which includes Holy
Disorder youth service, two evening open youth
clubs, 20s/30s House group; oversees Sunday youth
groups, monthly youth service, schools work,
posters/visual communication.

Mr David Lucas
Norwich Community Church,
Fishergate Christian Centre,
Fishergate, Norwich, Norfolk NR3 1SE
Tel 01603 765795
Fax 01603 761222

Youth Worker
Norwich Community Church (New Church)
Oversees 11-14s midweek youth club, 11-14s
Sunday teaching group, school assemblies and
monthly 11-18s Sunday morning meeting.

Mr Ryan Lynch
The Good Shepherd Mission,
17 Three Colts Lane, Bethnal Green,
London E2 6JL
Tel 0171 7393822

Youth Worker
The Good Shepherd Mission (Independent)
Face-to-face outreach with non-Christian 11-21s,
street and club-based work, schools work with Year
10/11 students. Management and supervision of two
club-based volunteer teams.

Ms Cilla McKenna
Leith Methodist Church, Acorn Christian
Centre, Junction Place, Edinburgh EH6
Tel 0131 5537877

Youth Worker
Leith Methodist Church
Co-ordinates and guides the church youth work,
setting up an after-school study centre and club.

Mr John McLaren
49 Garden Street, Newton, Hyde,
Cheshire SK14 4AU
Tel 0161 368 0889

Schools & Youth Worker
New Life Church, Ashton-Under-Lyne (Independent)
Leads and trains a PAIS Project Schools Team,
running lunchtime clubs, assemblies and lessons.
Work within the church includes an open youth club
(11-19s) and discipling groups.

Mr Graham Marsh
Cranbrook, St John's Road, Belton,
Great Yarmouth, Norfolk NR31 9JT
Tel 01493 782206

Youth Pastor
King's Church (New Frontiers)
Co-ordinates and oversees youth and children's work
with specialist involvement with High and Middle
Schools in the Yarmouth and Waveney areas.

Mrs Mandy Marsh
St Peter's & St Paul's Church Centre,
Church Lane, Tonbridge, Kent TN9 1HD
Tel 01732 770962
Fax 01732 358052

Youth Minister
Tonbridge Parish Church (Church of England)
Oversees all work with 11-19s in six churches in the
parish, trains and encourages youth leaders and
schools work in one local school. Also detached
ministry with Ember Trust Bus on a local estate.

Miss Rosemary Maskell
12 Downfields, Welwyn Garden City,
Hertfordshire AL8 6XR
Tel 01707 321097

Youth Worker
St Francis of Assisi (Church of England)
Oversees young people's work within the church,
including youth services. Committed to weekly
detached street work locally. Schools and college
work and contact with uniformed organisations.

Mr Frank Meaden
40 Inverary Avenue, Pittelichar,
Glenrothes, Fife KY7 4QN
Tel 01592 773558

Evangelist
Glenrothes Church of Christ
Outreach among teenage and young adults.
Responsible for the organisation of various activities
designed to appeal to today's youth in a godly
setting.

Mr Mark Meardon
The Vicarage, Church Lane, Warfield,
Bracknell, Berkshire RG42 6EE
Tel 01344 882228

Youth Pastor/Worker
St Michael's (Church of England)
Oversees and runs a youth congregation, also
schools work and friendship evangelism, focused
on 12-18s.

Mr Bob Morris
Church House, 1 Woodland Close,
Thornhill, Southampton, Hampshire
SO18 5RD
Tel 01703 462257

Youth Pastor
Thornhill Baptist Church
Co-ordinates and develops the youth programme,
including evangelism and discipleship and pastoral
care of young people and their families. Also schools
work and developing leadership training.

Mr Andrew Mulcock
36 Whipton Lane, Exeter, Devon
EX1 3DS
Tel 01392 218739

Youth Co-ordinator
Isla Christian Fellowship (New Church)
Co-ordinates a programme of activities for young
people in five congregations and oversees their
discipleship. Also develops outreach activities to
teenagers in Exeter.

Mr Courtney Nangle
West Bridgford Baptist Church, Melton
Road, West Bridgford, Nottingham
NG2 7NF
Tel 0115 981 0690

Youth Pastor
West Bridgford Baptist Church
Responsible for all aspects of work with 11-18s
within the church and community and the ongoing
recruiting and training of volunteer leaders. Also
involved in schools work.

Miss Gail Neill
45 Elmfield Road, Glengormley,
County Antrim BT36 6DN
Tel 01232 841644

Youth Worker
First Ballymoney Presbyterian Church
Leads young people's Bible study, youth fellowship
and youth club. Also visits young people connected
to the church.

Mr Ian Norman
19 Seggielea Road, Jordanhill, Glasgow
G13 1XJ
Tel 0141 954 7035
Fax 0141 959 2496
email ian.norman@strath.ac.uk

Youth Worker
Jordanhill Parish Church (Church of Scotland)
Co-ordinates and runs a youth programme which
ranges from Bible study groups to an open youth
cafe. Encourages team work.

Mr Russ Oliver
Generation Resource Centre,
Ruxley Lane, Epsom, Surrey KT19 0UY
Tel 0181 786 8221
Fax 0181 393 2916

Youth Team Leader
Generation (Pioneer)
Oversees, trains, and directs young people's team
working into youth clubs, schools, drop-in, events
and detached youth work.

Mr Don Palmer
4 Turners Croft, Heslington, York YO1 5EL
Tel 01904 431571

Church Worker
York Community Church (New Church)
Co-ordinates three Covenanters clubs. Local schools
work, including assemblies, classes and school
clubs.

Mr Clive Parnell
Davidson's Mains Parish Church, 1 Quality
Street, Edinburgh EH4
Tel 0131 312 6282

Youth Worker
*Davidson's Mains Parish Church (Church of
Scotland)*
Relational youth work through schools, youth clubs,
'Chillroom' and football. Overall co-ordination of the
church youth work, liaison with parents and teachers.

Mr Jerry Parr
142B High Street, Brentwood , Essex
CM14 4AT
Tel 01278 201184

Youth Minister
Brentwood Baptist Church
Responsible for young people, leaders, clubs and the
youth ministry vision to 11-18s. Also schools work
and inter-church townwide events.

Mr Neil Pattison
Manna Christian Fellowship, 13 Brewer
Street, Maidstone, Kent ME14 1RU
Tel 01622 757095
Fax 01622 751343

Youth & Schools Worker
Manna Christian Fellowship (Assembly of God)
Oversees and co-ordinates youth work in the church
for 11-18s. Also schools work in twelve local
secondary schools.

Mr David Pennie
9 Richmond Way, Loose, Maidstone, Kent
ME15 6BL
Tel 01622 674871

Youth Worker
Loose Baptist Church
Responsible for all youth work (11+), evangelism and
discipleship. Also leads lunchtime schools club, and
occasionally promotes concerts.

Mr Pip Piper
21 Alcester Road, Moseley, Birmingham
B13 8AR
Tel 0121 442 4484
Fax 0121 442 4345

Youth Pastor
Riverside Church (Independent New Church)
Responsible for the maintenance and development of the church's work among 11-18s, both in and outside of the church.

Mr Andy Poole
Beverley Minster Parish Office, Beverley Minster, Beverley, East Yorkshire HU17 0DP
Tel 01482 848540

Youth Leader
Beverley Minster (Church of England)
Has delegated oversight of the youth and children's work in the parish, with particular attention to those of secondary school age. Includes outreach through schools work.

Mr Chris Pope
1 Queen's Gardens, Tunbridge Wells, Kent TN2 3RX
Tel 01892 520440

Youth Pastor
Tunbridge Wells Baptist Church
Encourages young people to commit to Christ, discipling and training them to take an active part in the life and worship of the church, and in evangelism.

Mr Robert Poulesland
22 Barnett Place, Cleethorpes DN35 7SU
Tel 01472 698140

Youth Worker/Deanery Youth Advisor
St John's & St Stephen's (Church of England)
Responsible for a full-time open youth project. Trains and supervises voluntary and part-time staff, provides training and support for deanery youth workers. Also works in local senior schools.

Mr Andy Poultney
Good Shepherd Church, Collier Row Lane, Romford, Essex RM5 3BA
Tel 01708 745626
Fax 01708 726423

Youth Minister
Good Shepherd (Church of England)
Co-ordinates children's and youth work, including training of leaders, development of outreach to young people, schools work and liaising with other local youth ministers.

Mr David Pratt
Deeside Christian Fellowship Church, Binghill Drive, Milltimber, Aberdeen AB1 0JE
Tel 01224 733979
Fax 01224 734430

Youth Pastor
Deeside Christian Fellowship Church
Leadership of all areas of youth and children's work, including pastoral care. Also helps recruit and train volunteer leaders and promotes evangelistic activity among the young people.

Mrs Hannah Rayfield
St James & Emmanuel Parish Office, 6 Barlow Moor Road, Didsbury, Manchester M20 6TR
Tel 0161 455 7863
Fax 0161 445 1248

Children's and Youth Work Co-ordinator
St James & Emmanuel (Church of England)
Leads outreach, teaching, worship and social activities for and among teenagers. Also supports and trains leaders for work among 0-18s.

Mr Malcolm Reddaway
33 Pen-y-dre, Rhiwbina, Cardiff CF4 6EJ
Tel 01222 623791

Youth Worker
Rhiwbina Baptist Church
Oversees the church children's and youth
programmes and the training, equipping and
resourcing of the youth team. Extensive hands-on
work with 12-20s, including teaching, discipling and
open youth work.

Revd Steve Reilly
Bridge Street Pentecostal Church,
Bridge Street, Leeds LS2 7NX
Tel 0113 243 1375
Fax 0113 245 5452

Youth Pastor
Bridge Street Pentecostal Church (Elim)
Oversees the youth work among age 13-plus.

Mr Mike Resch
58 Drury Road, West Harrow, Middlesex
HA1 4BW
Tel 0181 423 1120/0973 764604

Parish Youth Worker
Christ Church Roxeth & St Peter's (Anglican)

Mr Robin Rolls
Emmanuel, 78 Brindley Street,
Hull HU9 3BT
Tel 01482 711008/0831 576952

Parish Youth Worker
Drypool Parish (Church of England)
Detached and relational work in schools, a youth
club, drop-in cafe, parks and on the streets. Also
nurtures Christians and trains volunteer workers.

Mr Stuart Ross
Potts Place, 11A West Street, Marlow,
Buckinghamshire SL7 2LS
Tel 01628 478988
Fax 01628 478987

Schools & Youth Worker
Marlow Christian Fellowship (New Church)
Oversees Saturday night youth club, youth holidays,
detached work and informal work at lunchtime in
schools.

Mr Danny Rosser
409 Victoria Road, South Ruislip,
Middlesex HA4 0EF
Tel 01956 255375

Youth Worker
St Paul's (Church of England)
Oversees and trains the church in detached and 'in-
house' youth work, including under-18s nightclub,
open youth group, youth celebration and two school
Christian Unions. Also oversees Warehouse
Ministries youth work training courses.

Mr Paul Sanderson
Surbiton Community Centre, The Retreat,
Surbiton, Surrey KT5 8RN
Tel 0181 296 9088
Fax 0181 296 9717

Youth & Children's Co-ordinator
The Community Church (Pioneer)
Co-ordinates and develops church-based discipling
projects in three congregations. Oversees relational
outreach in open youth clubs, detached and schools
work. Specialises in youth counselling in schools and
basketball coaching. Also DJing, playschemes and
chair of Shopfront Youth Advice & Counselling
Service in Kingston-upon-Thames.

Mr Jem Sewell
Slough Baptist Church, Windsor Road,
Slough, Berkshire SL3 7BX
Tel 01753 523058
Fax 01753 790728
email 100255.2055@compuserv.com

Assistant Pastor
Slough Baptist Church
Enables children's and youth work (0-18s) in and out
of the church. Special presentations to Year 6 pupils
in local schools at Christmas and Easter.

Mr Pete Shears
Greenford Baptist Church, Beechwood
Avenue, Greenford, Middlesex UB6 9UA
Tel 0181 813 2285

Youth Pastor
Greenford Baptist Church (Baptist/Pioneer)
Co-ordinates and oversees all youth programmes
and projects for 11-18s. Additional responsibility with
area-wide 'Back to Reality' project.

Miss Maggie Simpson
1 Church Street West, Woking,
Surrey GU21 1DJ
Tel 01483 714150
Fax 01483 725050

Youth & Schools Worker
The Coign Church (New Frontiers)
Oversees and leads the church youth work which
includes a Saturday programme, discipleship groups
and a non-alcoholic bar. Also schools work -
assemblies, Christian Unions and lunchtime clubs.

Mr Pall Singh
24 Oulton Road, Shirley, Solihull,
West Midlands B90 3NE
Tel 0121 744 3057
Fax 0121 744 2829

Youth Evangelist
Solihull Christian Fellowship (New Church)
Responsibility for the 11-18s in the church. Oversees
a youth leadership team, trains other youth leaders
through 'Youth Equip', works among Asian teenagers
in school.

Mr Paul Smit
102 Dudley Road, Tipton,
West Midlands DY4 8DL
Tel 0121 557 2106
Fax 01902 883221

Youth Pastor
Vineyard Christian Fellowship (Independent)
Responsible for reaching and keeping 11-18s,
including discipleship and taking them on short-term
outreach.

Mr Gary Smith
557 Gander Green Lane, North Cheam,
Sutton, Surrey SM3 9RF
Tel 0181 641 5872

Youth Pastor
North Cheam Baptist Church
Oversees the church's work with 5-18s. Trains
volunteer leaders and helpers, runs youth
discipleship and 'Just Looking' groups.

Mr Norman Smith
23 Kingsland Road, Broadwater,
Worthing, West Sussex BN14 9EB
Tel 01903 212153

Parish Youth Worker
Broadwater Parish (Church of England)
Co-ordinates the children's and youth work in three
churches, including open youth club and schools
work in five local schools; trains volunteers.
Alternative worship services and preaching and
leading at all-age and adult church services.

Mr Tony Stephen
Pitmachie, Arbeadie Terrace, Banchory
AB31 3TN
Tel 01330 824876
Fax 01330 824876
email 100777.1021@compuserve.com

Youth Co-ordinator
Banchorny Ternan East/West (Church of Scotland)
Co-ordinates joint youth programme for 12-18s,
recruiting and training volunteers, team building,
schools work, worship initiatives, pastoral contact
with young people and parents.

Mr David Stewart
Queen's Cross Church, Albyn Place,
Aberdeen AB1 1UN
Tel 01224 644742
email brigodon@wintermute.co.uk

Youth Worker
Queen's Cross Church (Church of Scotland)
Developing the church outreach to teens and young
adults, encouraging youth/young adult involvement in
the life and worship of the church. Also develops and
trains leaders.

Mr Tim Stillwell
Holy Trinity Brompton, Brompton Road,
London SW7 1JA
Tel 0171 581 8255
Fax 0171 589 3390

Youth Leader
Holy Trinity Brompton (Church of England)
Recruits, trains and oversees the youth team to teach
and disciple 11-18s. Schools work includes
assemblies and Christian Unions. Arranges youth
weekends/weeks away for teaching, ministry and fun.
Also organises and resources 'Youth Alpha' courses
for the church and elsewhere.

Mrs Georgina Taylor
327 New Hey Road, East Bowling,
Bradford BD4 7LD
Tel 01274 726952

Youth Co-ordinator
St John's (Church of England)
Co-ordinates the church youth small groups (cell
groups), manages the drop-in centre and Youth
Outreach Strategy. Also streetwork, schools work,
informal education, small groups, discussion-based
groups among 15-25s.

Ms Roz Thachrah
The Good Shepherd Mission,
17 Three Colts Lane, Bethnal Green,
London E2 6JL
Tel 0171 739 3372

Youth & Community Worker
Good Shepherd Mission (Independent)
Face-to-face outreach with young people (9-21s) with
special responsibility for girls work, involving two
open club-based volunteer teams, teaching in
secondary schools, pastoral and counselling work.

Mr Andy Thompson
33 The Hill, Cromford, Nr Matlock,
Derbyshire DE4 3RF
Tel 01629 823310

Youth Worker
Holy Trinity, Matlock Bath (Church of England)
Oversees 5-18s programmes, schools work; recruits
and trains volunteer workers.

Ms Mandy Toms
9 Fletcher Grove, Penicuik, Midlothian
EH26 0JT

Youth Worker
Penicuik Churches Youth Project (Ecumenical)
Outreach to unchurched youth and co-ordinating the
church youth groups (11-18s). Also recruits and
trains adult volunteers.

Mr Paul Ward
8A Darling Road, Brockley,
London SE4 1YG
Tel 0181 691 3886

Youth Development Worker/Youth Pastor
The Barn (Ichthus)
Oversees a youth congregation of 14-19s, helps to
run a one-year youth work training course and is
developing a youth and schools work network across
the boroughs of South-East London.

Mr Alan Webb
The Salvation Army, Bayhall Road,
Tunbridge Wells, Kent
Tel 01892 535297

Youth Worker
The Salvation Army
Oversees all work among 13-25s; works with other
Christian youth workers in schools and townwide
events. Also works alongside Kent County Council on
detached youth work.

Mr Paul Weston
54A Hatherley Road, Sidcup,
Kent DA14 4AS
Tel 0181 309 5613/0956 558835
Fax 0181 309 6056

Youth Worker/Evangelist
New Generation Church (Pioneer)
Oversees youth team in all aspects of youth work
and schools ministry, including youth clubs and
outreach projects. Also works with the local council
and police.

Mr Ian White
5 Victoria Road, Diss, Norfolk IP22 3EY
Tel 01379 643580

District Youth Evangelist
Methodist Church
Preaching, teaching, schools work, evangelism
training, development of alternative worship, youth
retreats, courses and pilgrimages.

Miss Kathryn White
254 Ringwood Road, Ferndown,
Dorset BH22 9AR
Tel 01202 894004

Trainee Youth Worker
St Mary's & Glenmoor (Church of England)
Disciples and nurtures through midweek youth
groups, encouraging young people to make an
impact in their community.

Mr Stephen Whyatt
29 Beach Road, Cottenham,
Cambridge CB4 4RG
Tel 01223 237402

Youth Director
Histon Baptist Church
Responsible for all aspects of youth work (11+) within
the church and community.

Mr Tim Williamson
Godmanchester Baptist Church, East
Chadley Lane, Godmanchester,
Cambridgeshire PE18 8BJ
Tel 01480 458565
Fax 01480 458565

Youth Worker
Godmanchester Baptist Church
Responsible for the oversight of the church youth
work (11-25s) and the support and training of 24
volunteer leaders. Youth work includes open youth
club, young people's cell groups, inter-church youth
events and schools work. Also involved in training 13-
17s in children's work.

Mr David Willis
11 May Street, Bootle,
Merseyside
L20 5BE
Tel 0151 933 5027

Youth Pastor
Orrell Park Baptist Church
Encourages, trains and plans for youth and children's work with two emphases: pastoral care and evangelistic outreach. Is developing the work to reach into the community and local schools.

Mr Simon Wong
King's Church, 288 Priory Road,
Hastings, East Sussex TN34 3NN
Tel 01424 722133
Fax 01424 425344

Youth Pastor
King's Church (New Frontiers)
Oversees the church youth work (11-19s) and the training, pastoral oversight and equipping of two teams of youth leaders. Also co-ordinates youth events within the county alongside other churches.

Mr Matthew Woodhouse
62 Frederick Street, Waddesdon,
Aylesbury, Buckinghamshire HP18 0LX
Tel 01296 651586
Fax 01296 651476

Youth Worker
Aylesbury Vale Community Church
Reaching and keeping 8-19s, schools work in 21 local schools, out-of-school clubs for Christian and not-yet-Christian youth. Also trains volunteer workers.

Mr Stacey & Mrs Wendy Wyncoll
204 High Street, Wickham Market,
Woodbridge, Suffolk IP13 0RF
Tel 01728 747803

Youth Pastors
Wickham Market Gospel Hall (Brethren)
Lead and organise all church youth and children's meetings (5-18s) for outreach and teaching, schools work and occasional special outreach events/missions. Also responsible for family services.

Miss Sara Wynne
Youth Link, Manor Park Christian Centre,
454 High Street North, Manor Park,
London E12 6RH
Tel 0181 470 9930
Fax 0181 503 4033

Youth Co-ordinator & Schools Worker
Newham Christian Fellowships (Inter-denominational)
Overseees the youth work in the Borough of Newham, speaking at Christian Unions, schools work in local schools, visiting church youth groups, bringing local youth leaders together for fellowship and training. Also organises borough-wide events.

DENOMINATIONAL
YOUTH OFFICERS

Denominational youth officers offer a range of services which may include: consultancy, training, resources, guidance and advice on contacts and agencies which offer a range of services to encourage and equip church-based youth work.

Assemblies of God

Mr Peter Goulding

Youth Alive Ministries,
PO Box 43, Newtown,
Powys SY16 1WB

Baptist Union of Great Britain

Baptist House, PO Box 44,
129 Broadway, Didcot,
Oxfordshire
OX11 8RT
Tel 01235 512077
Fax 01235 811537
email 100442.1750@compuserve.com

Mr Iain Hoskins
Youth Adviser to the Baptist Union of Great Britain
The mission of Baptist Union Youth Ministry is to provide spiritual and professional support to young people, and those who work with them, within the Baptist fellowship, raising the issues and perspectives of young people. The youth office produces/organises a journal for youth specialists, booklets and other resources, an annual conference and a recognition list of youth specialists.

South West Scotland Baptist Youth

64 Adamton Road North, Prestwick,
Ayrshire KA9 2ES
Tel 01292 477136
Fax 01292 477136

Mr Glen Cartwright
Youth Co-ordinator
Working together as Baptist youth in South-West Scotland to promote outreach; sharing people and resources and hightening the profile of youth.

Baptist Union of Ireland

Baptist Union of Ireland,
117 Lisburn Road, Belfast BT9 7AF
Tel 01232 663108
Fax 01232 663616

Mr Jackie Whyte
Youth Secretary, Baptist Youth
Provides activities, camps, evangelism teams, resources and training for children, young people and leaders of Irish Baptist churches.

Church in Wales

The Church in Wales Board of Mission (Youth Sector), Church in Wales Centre, Woodlands Place, Penarth, South Glamorgan, CF64 2EX
Tel 01222 705278
Fax 01222 712413

Ms Suzie Cole
Youth Officer
Advises, encourages and trains youth workers at diocesan and parish levels. Also maintains links with other Anglican provinces and with other youth officers within Wales.

Church of England

Church of England Youth Services
Great Smith Street, London SW1P 3NZ
Tel 0171 222 9011
Fax 0171 233 1094

National Youth Officers:
Mr Peter Ball
Ms Maxine Green

The Church of England supports a network of Youth Officers/Advisers in each diocese throughout England. The following entries give details of each diocesan contact.

Bath & Wells:
Mr Frank Nealis, Mr David Williamson, Miss Yvonne Criddle
The Old Deanery, Wells, Somerset BA5 2UG
Tel 01749 670777
Fax 01749 674240

Birmingham:
Mr S. Summers
Diocesan Office, 175 Harborne Park Road, Harborne, Birmingham B17 0BH
Tel 0121 427 5141
Fax 0121 428 1114

Blackburn:
Diocesan Office
Cathedral Close, Blackburn, Lancashire BB1 5AA
Tel 01254 54421

Bradford:
Diocesan Office, Cathedral Hall, Stott Hill, Bradford, West Yorkshire BD1 4ET
Tel 01274 676410

Bristol:
Revd Mark Pilgrim
Diocesan Church House, 23 Great George Street, Bristol, Avon BS1 5QZ
Tel 0117 921 4411
Fax 0117 934 9373

Canterbury:
Mrs Katie McDaniel
Diocesan House, Lady Wootton's Green, Canterbury, Kent CT1 1NQ
Tel 01227 459401
Fax 01227 450964

Carlisle:
Revd Ian Hay
Church House, West Walls, Carlisle,
Cumbria CA3 8UE
Tel 01228 38086

Chelmsford:
Diocesan Office, 53 New Street,
Chelmsford, Essex CM1 1AT
Tel 01799 522006

Chester:
Revd Helen Chantry
Diocesan Office, Raymond Street,
Chester CH1 4PN
Tel 01244 379222
Fax 01244 383835

Chichester:
Diocesan Church House, 211 New Church
Road, Hove, East Sussex BN3 4ED
Tel 01323 896014

Coventry:
Mr Stephen Tash
The Vicarage, Salford Priors, Evesham,
Worcestershire WR11 5UX
Tel 01789 772445
Fax 01789 772445

Derby:
Revd Christine Dyer
Derby Church House, Full Street, Derby
DE1 3DR
Tel 01332 382233
Fax 01332 291988

Durham:
Auckland Castle, Bishop Auckland,
County Durham DL14 7QJ
Tel 0191 384 3692

Ely:
Diocesan Office, Bishop Woodford House,
Barton Road, Ely, Cambridgeshire
CB7 4DX
Tel 01353 663579

Exeter:
Captain Tony Williams
The Rectory, Ideford, Newton Abbot,
Devon TQ13 0BA
Tel 01626 852828
Fax 01626 852828
email ajw1306@aol.uk

Gloucester:
Church House, College Green, Gloucester
GL1 2LY
Tel 01452 410022

Guildford:
Revd Karina Green
Educational Centre, The Cathedral,
Guildford, Surrey GU2 5UP
Tel 01483 450423
Fax 01483 450424

Hereford:
Diocesan Office, The Palace, Hereford
HR4 9BL
Tel 01584 872334

Leicester:
Church House, 3-5 St Martin's East,
Leicester LE1 5FX
Tel 0116 262 7445

Lichfield:
St Mary's House, The Close, Lichfield,
Staffordshire, WS13 7LD
Tel 01543 414551

YOUTH OFFICERS

Lincoln:
Captain David Rose
Forum Office, Church House, Old Palace,
Lincoln LN2 1PU
Tel 01522 528886
Fax 01522 512717

Liverpool:
Church House, 1 Hanover Street, Liverpool
L1 3DW
Tel 0151 709 9722

London:
Diocesan House, 34 Causton Street,
London SW1P 4AU

Manchester:
Church House, 90 Deangate, Manchester
M3 2GH
Tel 0161 834 1022

Newcastle:
Mr Neal Terry
Denewood, Clayton Road, Newcastle-
Upon-Tyne NE2 1TL
Tel 0191 281 9930
Fax 0191 281 1452

Norwich:
Diocesan House, 109 Dereham Road,
Easton, Norwich, Norfolk DR9 5ES
Tel 01603 881352

Oxford:
Diocesan Church House, North Hinksley,
Oxford OX2 0NB
Tel 01865 244566

Peterborough:
The Palace, Peterborough, Cambridgeshire
PE1 1YB
Tel 01604 751907

Portsmouth:
Cathedral House, St Thomas Street,
Portsmouth, Hampshire PO1 2HA
Tel 01705 822053

Ripon:
Diocesan Office, St Mary's Street, Leeds
LS9 7DP
Tel 0113 248 7487

Rochester:
St Nicholas' Church, Boley Hill,
Rochester, Kent ME1 1SL
Tel 01634 843667

St Albans:
Mr David Green
Diocesan Educational Centre, Hall Grove,
Welwyn Garden City, Hertfordshire
AL7 4PJ
Tel 01707 335968
Fax 01707 373089

St Edmondsbury & Ipswich:
Diocesan House, 13-15 Tower Street,
Ipswich, Suffolk IP1 3BG
Tel 01473 216944

Salisbury:
Captain Paul Niemiec
Board of Education, 97 Crane Street,
Salisbury, Wiltshire SP1 2QA
Tel 01722 411977

Sheffield:
Diocesan Church House,
95-99 Effingham Street, Rotherham,
South Yorkshire S65 1BL
Tel 01709 837547

Sodor & Man:
Revd Roderick Geddes
The Rectory, Village Road, Kirk Andreas,
Isle of Man IM7 4HH
Tel 01624 880419

Southwark:
Diocesan Office, Trinity House,
4 Chapel Court, Borough High Street,
London SE1 1HN
Tel 0181 6815496/7

Southwell:
Dunham House, Westgate, Southwell,
Nottinghamshire NG25 0JL
Tel 01636 814504

Truro:
Diocesan House, Kenwyn, Truro,
Cornwall TR1 3DU
Tel 01872 74352

Wakefield:
Revd Rob Whitehouse
Wakefield Diocese Youth Department,
191 Bickby Road, Wakefield, West
Yorkshire HD2 2BX
Tel 01484 424071
Fax 01484 424071
email 100530.1135@compuserve.com

Winchester:
Church House, 9 The Close, Winchester,
Hampshire SO23 9LS
Tel 01962 844644

Worcester:
The Old Palace, Deansway, Worcester
WR1 2JE
Tel 01905 20537/8

York:
Mr Graham Richards
54 York Road, Tadcaster, North Yorkshire
LS24 8AF
Tel 01937 832375/0374 495773
Fax 01937 832375

Church of Scotland

Church of Scotland Board of Parish
Education,
20 Inverleith Terrace, Edinburgh EH3 5NS
Tel 0131 332 0343
Fax 0131 315 2161
email 101331.627@compuserve.com

Mr Steve Mallon
National Youth Advisor
Publishes curriculum materials for use with 12-15s
and young adults; runs training courses and training
events for youth workers. Also supports full-time
youth workers in local churches.

Church of Scotland, 59 Elmbank Street,
Glasgow G2 4PQ
Tel 0141 333 9374
Fax 0141 333 9374

Dr Kathy Hooke
Glasgow Presbytery Youth Advisor

Congregational Federation

Congregational Federation Youth,
Fieldhead, Wilsden Road, Harden,
Bingley, West Yorkshire BD16 1JN
Tel 01535 274079

Revd Robert Waddington
National Youth Co-ordinator
Co-ordinates youth activities within the
Congregational Federation, including training for
churches and area organisations in youth matters.

Elim Church

On Target
Elim National Youthwork, Bridge Street
Church, Bridge Street, Leeds LS2 7NX
Tel 0113 243 1375
Fax 0113 245 5452

Mr Steve Reilly
National Youth Co-ordinator
Missions, training in youth work, communicating to
youth.

Methodist

Methodist Association of Youth Clubs
(MAYC)
2 Chester House, Pages Lane, Muswell
Hill, London N10 1PR
Tel 0181 444 9845
Fax 0181 365 2687

Revd Mark Wakelin
National Secretary

Methodist Church in East Anglia
5 Victoria Road, Diss, Norfolk IP22 3EY
Tel 01379 643580

Revd Malcolm Brady
District Youth Evangelist
Evangelism among 13-25s through schools, youth
clubs, retreats, missions and worship.

Methodist Church in Ireland Department
of Youth & Children's Work
Aldersgate House, University Road,
Belfast BT7 1NA
Tel 01232 327191

Presbyterian Church

Presbyterian Church of Wales Youth Service
Coleg Y Bala, Ffrydan Road, Bala,
Gwynedd LL23 7RY
Tel 01678 520565
Fax 01678 520565

Revd Bryn Williams
Director of Youth Service
Proclaims the gospel to children and young people
throughout Wales and helps to develop the whole
person - mentally, physically and spiritually.

Presbyterian Youth Board
Church House, Fisherwick Place, Belfast
BT1 6DW

Miss Roz Stirling
Youth Officer
Envisions the denomination on the needs of young
people, the culture they live in and the role of the
church in ministering to them.

YOUTH OFFICERS

Roman Catholic Church

Westminster:
SPEC All Saints Pastoral Centre, Shenley
Lane, London Colney, Hertforshire AL2
1AQ

Arundel and Brighton:
Ms Joanna Stevens & Mr Peter Siney
Diocesan Youth Office, Christian Education
Centre, 4 Southgate Drive, Crawley , West
Sussex RH10 6RP

Birmingham:
Revd Andy Ison
Diocesan Youth Officer, Dwyer House,
37 Victoria Road, Acocks Green,
Birmingham B27 7XZ

Brentwood:
Diocesan Youth Service, Cathedral House,
28 Ingrave Road, Brentwood, Essex CM15
8AT

Clifton:
Ms Mary McGinty
Diocesan Youth Officer, Clifton Diocesan
Offices, St Nicholas House,
Lawford's Gate, Bristol BS5 0RE

Hallam:
Revd Kevan Grady
Diocesan Youth Chaplain, St Charles'
Pastoral Centre, St Charles' Street,
Sheffield S9 3W0

Lancaster:
Ms Anne Kennedy
Diocesan Youth Officer, Education Centre,
Cathedral Buildings, Balmoral Road,
Lancaster LA1 3BT

Leeds:
Revd Nick Farrell
Diocesan Youth Service, 5 St Mark Avenue,
Leeds LS2 9BN

Liverpool:
Revd Tony Frain
Leyfield House, Honeys Green Lane,
Liverpool L12 9HY

Middlesbrough:
Sr Lorraine Miller
Curial Offices, 50a The Avenue, Linthorpe,
Middlesborough, Cleveland TS5 6QT

Northampton:
Revd Michael Harrison
Diocesan Youth Office, 71 Occupation
Road, Corby, Northamptonshire
NN17 1EE

Nottingham:
Revd Gregory Tobin
Diocesan Youth Director, The Briars
Residential Training Centre, Crich
Common, Matlock, Derbyshire DB4 5BW

Portsmouth:
Ms Julie Meads
Diocesan Youth Office, Park Place
Pastoral Centre, Winchester Road,
Wickham, Hampshire PO17 5HA

Salford:
Ms Theresa Davies
Diocesan Youth Officer, Diocesan Youth
Office, 5 Gerald Road, Pendleton, Salford,
Lancashire M6 6DL

Shrewsbury:
Revd Tony Leonard
Diocesan Youth Chaplain, St Peter's,
Firbank Road, Newall Road ,
Wythenshaw, Manchester M23 8YS

Southwark:
Revd Chris Connor
Diocesan Youth Chaplain, Southwark
Catholic Youth Service, 135 Nightingale
Lane, London SW12 8NE

Wrexham:
Rt Revd E. Regan
Bishop of Wrexham, Bishop's House,
Sontley Road, Wrexham, Clwyd LL13 7EW

Salvation Army

Salvation Army Youth Department,
Territorial Youth Department, William
Booth Memorial College, Denmark Hill,
London SE5 8BQ
Tel 0171 738 5533
Fax 0171 738 6091

Major Ray Bates
Territorial Youth Secretary
Provides support, training and resources for youth
work undertaken by the Salvation Army in the United
Kingdom.

United Reformed Church

United Reformed Church, 86 Tavistock
Place, London WC1H 9RT
Tel 0171 916 2020
Fax 0171 916 2021

Mr Paul Franklin
National Youth Secretary
Promotes imaginative youth work in all areas of
church life, responds to the needs of young people
and youth workers and interprets these to the church
and the church's needs to them.

Northern & Yorkshire:
Miss Janet Turner
7 Lennox Avenue, Richmond, North
Yorkshire DL10 5AF

North Western:
Mr Leo Roberts
173b Worsley Road, Winton , Eccles,
Greater Manchester M30 8LY

Mersey:
Mr John Brown
5 Brentnall Close, Great Thankley,
Warrington , Cheshire WA5 1XN

East Midlands:
Mr John Quilter
14 Northampton Road, Yardley Hastings,
Northamptonshire NN7 1EX

West Midlands:
Mr Wallie Warmington
271 Rotten Park Road, Edgbaston,
Birmingham, West Midlands B16 0LP

Eastern:
Mr Henry Playle
United Reformed Church, Province Office,
5 Pound Hill, Cambridge CB3 0AE

South Western:
Mr Ivan Andrews
23 Carlton Road, Broadfields, Exeter,
Devon EX2 5NS

Wessex:
Miss Ann Martin
Flat 3 Holt Lodge, Northlands Road,
Southampton, Hampshire SO1 2LJ

Thames North:
Mrs Sandra Ackroyd
96 Dowlands Park Road, Tottenham,
London N17 6PA

Southern:
Miss Wendy Walker
22 Lancelot Close, Ifield, Crawley, West
Sussex RH11 0PG

Wales:
Mr Colin Capewell
Persondy, Trallong, Brecon, Powys LD3
8HP

YOUTH OFFICERS

YOUTH MINISTRY
SPECIALISTS AND TRAINERS

Including Schools Workers, Youth Evangelists, Youth Work Trainers, Youth Ministry Trusts and some Para-Church Youth Workers.

Mr John Allan
23 Raleigh Road, Exeter,
Devon EX1 1TQ
Tel 01392 411691
Fax 01392 411691
email john@aware.telme.com

Mr John Allan
Youthwork Trainer
No set fee
Trains in all aspects of youth work, especially church-based; willing to consult and advise as time permits.

Ashford Youth Focus
5 Hardey Close, Wilesborough, Ashford,
Kent, TN24 0XB

Mr Roger Whitely

Back to Reality
c/o Greenford Baptist Church,
Beechwood Avenue, Greenford,
Middlesex UB6 9UA
Tel 0181 813 2285

Mr Pete Shears
Co-ordinator
Ealing area team co-ordinating youth celebrations, social action projects and evangelism for local church youth work.

Becomers UK
PO Box 9752, Renfrew, Glasgow
PA4 8EL
Tel 0141 616 0798
Fax 0141 616 0798

Ms Susan Lennartson
Director/Counsellor
Trains group facilitators, counsels abuse victims, facilitates support groups, speaks and helps promote a positive biblical response to issues of abuse.

Big Ideas
PO Box 39, Penarth, South Glamorgan
CF64 2YH
Tel 01222 382462
Fax 01222 382462

Mr Nigel James/Mr Gary Smith
Directors
£150 day/£150 eve
Exploring relevant ways of communicating the Christian faith to young people using live music, big screen video, chat and humour.

The Boot Brothers
Christian Centre, 104 Talbot Street,
Nottingham NG1 5GL
Tel 0115 950 4506
Fax 0115 950 4506

Mr Jospeh Boot
Evangelist
£150 day / £100 eve
A Christian band/ministry team available for all kinds
of evangelistic activities. Also involved in
teaching/training weekends and full conference
programmes (Assemblies of God).

The Bridge Project
The Bridge, The Annex, St Michael's
Community Centre, St Michael's Road,
Salisbury, Wiltshire SP2 9LZ
Tel 01722 410746

Mr John Baxter-Brown

Bridges Project
143 Karlaxton Road, Grantham,
Lincolnshire NG31 7AG
email 100013.3720@compuserve.com

Mr Mark Ainsworth

Mr Danny Brierley
Altrincham Baptist Church, Hale Road,
Altrincham, Cheshire WA14 2EW
Tel 0161 941 2018
Fax 0161 941 2064

Mr Danny Brierley
Youth Ministry Trainer
£100 day / £50 eve
External training to Altrincham Baptist Church only
undertaken if it is of benefit to the region of North-
West England.

Christian Education in Nottingham Schools (CENS)
232 Westdale Lane, Carlton, Nottingham
NG5 2GS
Tel 0115 960 6228

Mr Chris Chesterton
Director
Schools work in Nottinghamshire, plus training and
provision of quality resource material.

Christian Warriors
Christian Centre, Temple Street,
Wolverhampton, West Midlands WV2 4AQ
Tel 01902 710902
Fax 01902 714469

Mr Steven Uppal
Director
£75 day / £40 eve
Aims to equip the saints and save the lost. Uses the
creative arts and modern technology to communicate
the gospel. Also provides training in various aspects
of youth ministry.

The Christians in Schools Trust
5 Siskin Road, Offerton, Stockport,
Cheshire SK2 5SX
Tel 0161 487 4431

Mr Steve Bullock
Secondary Schools Worker
Establishes, maintains and develops a Christian
presence in schools through the encouragement,
training and resourcing of teachers and pupils.

SPECIALISTS AND TRAINERS

Craven Area Inter-School Christian Union

7 Kendal Close, Hellifield, Skipton
BD23 4HG
Tel 01729 850680

Ms Claire Whittle
Schools Worker
Area-wide schools work in mainly secondary and middle schools on behalf of local churches, taking assemblies, lessons and Christian Union groups. Also organises regular residential holidays. Overseen by North-West Evangelistic Trust.

The Crops Trust

68a Westgate, Peterborough PE1 1RG
Tel 01733 352701
Fax 01733 352701

Mr Richard Morrison
Director
Work with churched and unchurched youth, schools work and leadership resourcing and training in the Peterborough area.

Dacorum Churches Schools Liaison Officer Trust

Marlowes Methodist Church, Marlowes, Hemel Hempstead, Hertfordshire HP1 1LB
Tel 01442 246850

Miss Rachel Dutton
Schools Worker
Works in eight secondary schools, taking assemblies, teaching RE, running lunchtime and after school clubs. Also forges links between schools and churches.

The Damascus Trust

20 Woodfield Road, Braintree, Essex
CM7 3HZ
Tel 01376 342529
Fax 01376 342892

Mr Andy Paine
Director/Evangelist
Evangelistic agency working in partnership with local churches to enthuse and enable Christians for evangelism and establish ongoing outreach within church life. Work includes development of prayer, evangelism and nurture teams within local churches and heading up outreach events for young people/adults.

Mrs Linda Dunnett

44 Forfar Avenue, Glasgow G52 3JQ
Tel 0141 883 5956

Mrs Linda Dunnett
Youth Ministry Trainer
£25 day/£10 eve (No fee for local training events)
Trains youth leaders and potential leaders in reaching and keeping 11-19s throughout Scotland.

Exeter ICE Project

c/o YMCA, 41 St David's Hill, Exeter, Devon EX1 3AR
Tel 01392 411116

Mr Colin Piper

Exousia Trust

PO Box 437, Reading, Berkshire
RG30 3DF

Mr Sean Stillman
Evangelist
Expenses plus any gift
Encourages Christian teens to develop their faith so they can make a difference in their world. Takes the gospel among those whom the mainstream church would not normally reach.

Generation
Ruxley Lane, Epsom , Surrey KT19 0UY
Tel 0181 786 8221
Fax 0181 393 2916

Mr Russ Oliver
Team Leader
Runs a number of initiatives which include the
process of relationship-building, salvation,
discipleship, etc. Works in schools, discipleship
groups, large-scale youth events.

God's Squad
Christian Motorcycle Club UK,
PO Box 437, Reading RG30 3DF

Revd John Smith
International President
Offers assistance to the church in any ways
appropriate, bearing in mind the particular
attractiveness of the bike image to youth who may
not normally relate to church or other traditional
institutions.

Hands and Feet Trust
27 Forest Street, Kirkby-in-Ashfield,
Nottinghamshire NG17 7DT
Tel 01623 750978

Mr & Mrs Nigel & Jo Pimlott
Project Directors
£100 day / £100 eve
Youth and schools work with 11-18s. Also training
and development of youth workers, writing and
production of music, drama and resources.

Mr Geoff Harley-Mason
Youth Office, St Lawrence House, 1717
High Street, Knowle, Solihull, West
Midlands B93 0LN
Tel 01564 778802
Fax 01564 779123

Mr Geoff Harley-Mason
Youth Ministry Trainer
Trains leaders of 11-14s youth groups in nurture,
evangelism, teaching and youth-related issues.

Harrow Churches Schools Link Trust
Youth Office, Stanmore Baptist Church,
Abercorn Road, Stanmore,
Middlesex HA7 2PH
Tel 0181 9545281

Miss Heather Boyd
Schools Worker
A resource to local schools when they wish a
Christian from the community to take assemblies,
lessons and clubs. The Trust has established links
with local churches. Also involved in training
volunteer workers.

Headway Youth
36 Belmont Road, Luton, Bedfordshire
LU1 1LL
Tel 01582 401454

Mr Michael Hall
Youth Work Co-ordinator
Youth ministry, teaching and fellowship for young
people aged 15-29. A youth arm of the Methodist
Evangelical Movement Headway.

Mr Dellwyn Jones
28 St David's Way, Caerffili,
Mid Glamorgan CF83 1EY
Tel 01222 882726

Mr Dellwyn Jones
Youth Work Trainer
Through training, advice and support, the
encouragement and enabling of Christians to use
their giftings and calling for Christian youth work in
their community.

SPECIALISTS AND TRAINERS

Leeds Faith in Schools
16 Sunset Road, Leeds LS6 4LH
Tel 0113 275 6152

Mr Lee Jackson
Schools Worker
Full-time secondary schools worker in Leeds.

Mr Steve Legg
48 Conbar Avenue, Rustington,
Littlehampton, West Sussex BN16 3LY
Tel 07000 778779
Fax 01903 771672

Mr Steve Legg
Escapologist
£250 day / £175 eve
Uses escapology to challenge and help young
people to understand how Christ can set them free.
Work includes schools, colleges, universities, youth
groups and special services.

Mr Paul Loader
3 Cleve Road, Knowle, Bristol BS4 2JR
Tel 0117 977 2206

Mr Paul Loader
Singer/Evangelist (Baptist)
£50 day / £50 eve plus travel expenses
Communicates the Christian message to young
people through contemporary methods, including
concerts, multi-media magazine shows, etc. Also
preaches/teaches, youth missions, house parties and
schools work.

Logos Ministries
147 Albertbridge Road, Belfast BT5 4PS
Tel 01232 458362
Fax 01232 768344

Mr Thomas McClean
Director
Reaches young people with the claims and
challenges of Jesus through youth and schools
outreach. Also involved in motivating young people
into mission.

Marlow Youth Project
11A West Street, Marlow,
Buckinghamshire SL7 2LS
Tel 01628 478988
Fax 01628 478987

Mr Stuart Ross
Detached Youth Worker
Meets young people on their territory through street,
youth club and schools work.

Milton Keynes Bridgebuilder Trust
The David Baxter Centre, 63 North
Seventh Street, Central Milton Keynes,
Buckinghamshire MK9 2DP
Tel 01908 690555
Fax 01908 233335

Mr Tim Cutting
Schools Worker
Independent trust promoting Christian ministry in
local schools, including RE and other lessons,
Christian Unions and other groups. Communicates
the beliefs and message of the Christian faith and
equips other Christians to do the same.

Nightlife Project
84 Cranby Close, Weymouth, Dorset
DT4 0SS

Mr Paul Calvert

On The Edge
6 Park Close, Tiverton, Devon EX16 6AX
Tel 01884 253831

Mr Steve Bedford
Director

The Pais Project
Sharon Church, Brendon Avenue, Moston,
Manchester M40 9DN
Tel 0161 682 4646

Mr Paul Gibbs
National Director
£50 day / £40 eve
Training of schools and youth workers.

Mr Phillip Pittard
9 Ashenden Walk, Tunbridge Wells, Kent
TN2 3HR
Tel 01892 534261

Mr Phillip Pittard
Crusaders Kent Area Development Worker
Works with churches of all denominations to assist in
the launching and support of children's and youth
groups which aim to reach the unchurched.

Re:\build
4 Castle Grove, Oldswinford, Stourbridge,
West Midlands DY8 4HH
Tel 01384 440764
Fax 01384 440764
email 100451.254@compuserve.com

Mr Gerard & Mrs Chrissie Kelly
Co-Directors
£120 day / £60 eve
Promotes vision, action and prayer for the re-
evangelisation of secular Europe.

Revive
204 King Lane, Leeds LS17 6AA
Tel 0113 269 3742
Fax 0113 269 0722

Mr Simon Hall
Pastor
£30 day / £20 eve
A youth congregation based in a local Baptist church
which offers training in evangelism, youth worship
and church planting. This includes
training/experience days and/or weekends for young
people who want to explore creating their own
worship.

Ms Sue Rinaldi
44 High Street, Cobham, Surrey KT11 3EB
01932 867652
01932 867652

Ms Sue Rinaldi
Singer/Communicator
£160 day / £125 eve

The Rock Communion
236 Serbert Road, Forest Gate,
London E7 0NP
0181 5348500

Revd Simon Law
Leader
Presents a rock setting for the Anglican ASB Holy
Communion Service and organises workshops for
young people to participate and contribute to the
worship.

Rural Youth Work Project
5 Broad Lane, Upper Bucklebury, Nr
Reading, Berkshire RG7 5QH
Tel 01635 864683

Miss Michelle Fussell
Youth Worker
Rural youth work project which aims to meet the
needs of 11-25s in the rural West of Berkshire by
providing youth clubs, schools work, youth
celebrations and one-to-one work.

Mr James Sands
185 Rathkyle, Antrim, County Antrim
BT41 1LW
Tel 01849 460124

Mr James Sands
Youth Evangelist
Independent, inter-denominational youth evangelist
working with churches and youth groups. Also offers
training and advice.

Shalom Youth Project
Rutland Street, Grimsby DN32 7LT
Tel 01472 357107

Mr Robert Powlesland
Youth Worker
Christian informal education in a leisure setting using
open club work, group discussions, issue-based and
art/crafts, all age groups from 5-18s.

Shrewsbury Churches Youth Project
The Church Centre, Lancaster Road,
Shrewsbury SY1 3LE
Tel 01743 440512

Sister Pam Costin
Project Worker
An ecumenical project supported by Lichfield
Diocese, churches in Shrewsbury and the Church
Army. It is involved in schools work, church-based
youth work and various other aspects of youth
ministry in Shrewsbury.

Sidewalk (Scarborough Churches Detached Youth Work Project)
St Mary's Parish House, Castle Road,
Scarborough, North Yorkshire YO11 1HT
Tel 01723 500694

Mr Dave Ward
Senior Worker
£30 day
Aims to meet the needs of young people (13-25)
where they are through educating, enabling, training,
supporting and developing the whole person.

Mr Norman Smith
23 Kingsland Road, Broadwater, Worthing,
West Sussex BN14 9EB
Tel 01903 212153

Mr Norman Smith
Parish Youth Worker
Involved in five high schools, taking assemblies and
lessons; an ACET AIDS education instructor and
chaplain to Worthing Sea Scouts.

Solent Christian Trust
PO Box 200, Southampton, Hampshire
SO17 2DL
Tel 01703 315319
Fax 01703 315319
email 100302.3044@compuserve.com

Mr Nick Pollard
Director
£75 day / £75 eve plus travel
Evangelist working mainly in universities and sixth-
form colleges.

Spearhead
YMCA Kitto Centre, Honicknowle Lane,
Honicknowle, Plymouth, Devon PL5 3NG
Tel 01752 201918

Mr Andrew Gardiner
Chairman
Co-ordinates youth ministry in Plymouth on behalf of
over 40 churches. Organises events, leadership
training and youth outreach.

Stepps Youth Mission
Craigendmuir House, Cardowan Road,
Stepps, Glasgow G33 6AN
Tel 0141 779 2357

Mr Tom Greig
Bible and activity weekends, youth evangelism,
teaching, providing speakers for youth groups. Also
lends equipment and support to churches.

The 40:3 Trust
PO Box 403, Coventry CV3 6BR
Tel 01203 504792
Fax 01203 504792

Mr Mike Streeter
Director
£100 day / £50 eve
Itinerant evangelists working with local churches
nationwide to help them reach out to their area.

Urban Action, Manchester
Harpurhay United Church, Carisbrook
Street, Harpurhay, Manchester M9 1QR
Tel 0161 205 4388

Mr Dave Furze
Director

Viz-A-Viz
227 Rayleigh Road, Hutton, Brentwood,
Essex CM13 1PJ
Tel 01277 215222
Fax 01277 215222

Revd Dennis Pethers
Director
Evangelism training and presentation, working in
partnership with colleges, universities and churches
in presenting the gospel in relevant ways to people
today. Includes preaching, roadshows, training and
summer projects.

Mr Pete Ward
Old Mission Hall, 57b St Clements,
Oxford OX4 1AG
Tel 01865 722050
Fax 01865 201005
email peteyo@easynet.co.uk

Mr Pete Ward
Archbishop of Canterbury's Advisor for Youth Ministry

Warehouse Centre
7 Brook Road, Rayleigh, Essex SS6 7XX
Tel 01268 779999

Miss Alison Risdon
Youth Liaison Officer
Oversees youth outreach, including street work
among 11-17s. Also trains volunteers and works with
young people to improve their employment
prospects.

The Wavelength Trust
236 Serbert Road, Forest Gate,
London E7 0NP
Tel 0181 534 8500

Revd Simon Law
Worker
Promotes and encourages the Christian faith,
particularly among young people in secondary
schools and youth clubs.

What For Ministries
MAF Ingles Manor, Castle Hill Avenue,
Folkestone, Kent CT20 2TN
Tel 01303 238895

Mr Dave Barker

Without Fear Trust
80 South Street, Boness, West Lothian
EH81 9HA
Tel 01806 517055

Mr Stuart Fraser
Youth Worker
Enables local youth and adults to engage in youth
work with arts, recreation, discussion and other
relevant expressions, to share the gospel.

Word of Life Ministries (UK) Ltd
8 Beech Crescent, Larbert, Stirlingshire
FK5 3EY
Tel 01324 558535
Fax 01324 551442

Revd David Kelso
Director
Assists and serves local churches in the
evangelising, edifying and equipping of young people
for full-time and lay ministry.

Yeldall Christian Centres (Training Department)
Yeldall Manor, Hare Hatch, Reading,
Berkshire RG10 9XR
Tel 01734 401093
Fax 01734 404852

Mr Paul Roberts
Training Officer
£275 day / £50 eve
Trains youth workers in drug/alcohol awareness, how
and where to get help, how to promote drug
prevention programmes, basic drug counselling for
youth workers.

Youthlink
Manor Park Christian Centre, 454 High
Street North, Manor Park, London
E12 6RH
Tel 0181 470 9930
Fax 0181 503 4033

Miss Sara Wynne
Youth Co-ordinator and Schools Worker
Oversees the youth work in the London Borough of
Newham. Visits church youth groups, brings local
youth leaders together for fellowship and training,
organises borough-wide events and speaks at
Christian Unions, assemblies and RE lessons in the
local secondary schools.

Youth Ministries 2000
48 Birch House Road, Chesterton,
Newcastle-under-Lyme ST5 7HB
Tel 01782 866922

Mr Ian Hough
Evangelism Co-ordinator
Provides the opportunity for young people, either in
groups or as individuals, to come together to worship
God. Also makes youth work a priority in the area.

Agape

Fairgate House, King's Road, Tyseley,
Birmingham B11 2AA
Tel 0121 765 4404
Fax 0121 765 4065
email 100523645@compuserve.com

Mr David Wilson

Evangelism and discipleship in secondary schools,
universities and the business community. Discovery,
the schools ministry of Agape, reaches the 14-18s
through lessons, assemblies and follow-up of those
wanting to know more.

The Boys' Brigade

Felden Lodge, Hemel Hempstead,
Hertfordshire HP3 0BL
Tel 01442 231681
Fax 01442 235391

Mr Sydney Jones
Brigade Secretary
Christian uniformed youth work for boys aged 6-18.
Provides programmes, resource material and leader
training.

Brainstormers

87 Blackfriars Road, London SE1 8HA
Tel 0171 928 6538

Miss Tina Vygas
Administrator
Provides youth ministry training weekend and day
conferences. Organised jointly by Oasis Trust,
Youthwork magazine and Youth for Christ, the
November weekend conferences in Blackpool and
Eastbourne annually attract over 1,000 youth workers
for training, encouragement, worship, resources and
ideas.

Campaigners

Campaigner House, St Mark's Close,
Colney Heath, St Albans,
Hertfordshire AL4 0NQ
Tel 01727 824065

Revd Kenneth Argent
Director General

Careforce

577 Kingston Road, London SW20 8SA
Tel 0181 543 8671
Fax 0181 540 0013

Revd Ian Prior
Director
Serves evangelical churches and organisations in the
UK and Eire by placing Christian volunteers aged 18-
25 for 10-12 months where their help is most
needed. Placements can involve youth work, church
work, evangelistic outreach, residential carer, serving
in a rehabilitation centre.

Christian Aid

35 Lower Marsh, London SE1 7RT
Tel 0171 620 4444
Fax 0171 620 0719
email caid@gn.apc.org

Revd Michael Taylor
Director
The official development agency of 40 churches representing most denominations in the UK and Ireland. Working in over 60 countries worldwide, Christian Aid funds local church and other organisations overseas which fight poverty and help the poor become self-reliant. It also campaigns for a better deal for the poor from banks, big businesses and governments. Its Youth Advisers (Kevin McCullough and Jonathan Smith) provide training for youth leaders, assistance with events and the production of resources to increase the awareness among young people of global poverty and ways to take action to change the world.

Christian Endeavour

Wellesbourne House, Walton Road,
Wellesbourne, Warwick CV35 9JB
Tel 01789 470439

Christian Initiative on Teenage Sexuality

Care for the Family, 136 Newport Road,
Cardiff CF2 1DJ
Tel 01222 494431
Fax 01222 497807

Revd Jonathan Booth
Director
Networking and training and resourcing leadership, encouraging a biblical approach to sex and sexuality.

Christmas Cracker

5 Ethel Street, Birmingham B2 4BG
Tel 0121 633 0873
Fax 0121 633 0875
email 100620.11@compuserve.com

Mr Richard Wood
Project Director
Activates young people to put their faith into action, learn new skills, raise funds for the developing world and make an impact on their local community.

Church Youth Fellowships Association (CYFA)

Church Pastoral Aid Society, Athena Drive,
Tachbrook Place, Warwick CV34 6NG
Tel 01926 334242
Fax 01926 337613

Revd Steve Tilley
Head of CYFA
Bible-based resources, training and events for 14-18s and their leaders.

Covenanters

11/13 Lower Hillgate, Stockport,
Lancashire, SK1 1JQ
Tel 0161 474 1262

Mr Mark Tomlinson
Director

Cross Rhythms
PO Box 183, Plymouth , Devon PL3 4YN
Tel 01752 225623
Fax 01752 673441

Mr Chris Cole
Executive Officer
Produces Cross Rhythms magazine, which features
contemporary Christian music, news, reviews,
features and gigs. Also Cross Rhythms Festival,
which features music, arts and ministry.

Crusaders
2 Romeland Hill, St Albans, Hertforshire
AL3 4ET
Tel 01727 855422
Fax 01727 848518

Dr Alan Kerbey
National Director
National network of youth groups for outreach to
unchurched young people age 4-18. Supported by
teaching materials, leadership training, holidays,
events, and full-time area development workers.

(Northern Ireland) Crusaders
178 Cavehill Road, Belfast BT15 5EX
Tel 01232 712908
email 100760.3275@compuserve.com

Mr Hugh McCullough
N.I. Committee Member
An inter-denominational group reaching young
people for Jesus Christ to prepare them for
responsible Christian living and to develop their gifts
of leadership for tomorrow's world.

(Scottish) Crusaders
Challenge House, 29 Canal Street,
Glasgow
Tel 0141 331 2400
Fax 0141 332 8500

Mr Kevin Simpson
Director
Supports and resources over 50 youth groups
throughout Scotland which are reaching and
discipling unchurched young people (8-18s).

Frontier Youth Trust
70-74 City Road, London EC1Y 2BJ
Tel 0171 336 7744

Mr Michael Eastman
Secretary & Development Officer
A Christian network dedicated to advancing the
kingdom of God by supporting, resourcing and
training those working with and on behalf of
disadvantaged young people.

Frontier Youth Trust (England) Field
Officers:

North East
Mrs Jennie Appleby
FYT Office, 98 Dovecote Street,
Stockton-on-Tees TS18 1HA
Tel 01642 613991 (Tues/Wed only)

South West
Arkle Bell
FYT Office, 9-11 Clothier Road, Brislington,
Bristol, BS4 5RL
Tel 0117 971 3544

Yorks/Humbs
Chris Bristow
FYT Office, Fitzwilliam Centre, Fitzwilliam
Street, Sheffield S1 4JL
Tel 0114 272 1375

Midlands
Terry Dunnell
FYT Office, 59 Princes Road, Leicester
LE1 6TR

ORGANISATIONS

Executive Officer
Martin Hardwidge
The Manse, Grove Road, New Mill, Tring
HP23 5HA
Tel 0144 282 3142

London
Rana Johal
20 Amersham Road , New Cross, London
SE14 6QE
Tel 0181 694 8503

East
Tim Lovejoy
48 Harriet Martineau Close, Thetford,
Norfolk IP24 1UB
Tel 01842 764540

Frontier Youth Trust Northern Ireland
Mr Kenny Groves
Field Officer: N. Ireland
FYT Office, 157/9 Albertbridge Road,
Belfast BT5 4PS
Tel 01232 454806

Frontier Youth Trust Scotland
Ms Feri Salvesen
Administrator
Anderston Kelvingrove Church, 759b Argyle
Street, Glasgow G3 8DS
Tel 0141 204 4800

Frontier Youth Trust (Scotland)
Field Officers:

Western
Tom Britton
Anderston Kelvingrove Church,
759b Argyle Street, Glasgow G3 8DS
Tel 0141 204 4800

Eastern
Christine Pettie
Albany House, Meigle Street, Galashiels
TD1 1LN
Tel 01896 750526

Rob Frost Team
Raynes Park Methodist Church, Tolverne
Road, London SW20 8RA
Tel 0181 944 5678
Tel 0181 947 5152
email 100427.3310@compuserve.com

Revd Dr Rob Frost
National Evangelist for Methodist Church
Pioneer mission work, working alongside a church as part of a local vision to reach people for the Lord.

The Girls' Brigade (England & Wales)
62 Foxhall Road, Didcot, Oxfordshire
OX11 7BQ
Tel 01235 510425
Fax 01235 510429

Mrs Sylvia Bunting
National Secretary
Church-based uniformed youth/children's work with an evangelistic aim. The activity programme is aimed at holistic outreach; variety, challenge and development - helping girls to follow Jesus.

The Girls' Brigade in Scotland
Boys' Brigade House, 186 Bath Street,
Glasgow G2 4TQ
Tel 0141 332 1765
Fax 0141 331 2681

Miss Helen McLeod
Brigade Secretary
A uniformed organisation for girls, whose motto is
'seek, serve and follow Christ', which offers fun and
friendship, and a range of exciting activities to suit
girls from Primary 1 upwards.

Hope UK
25f Copperfield Street, London SE1 0EN
Tel 0171 928 0848
Fax 0171 401 3477

Mr George Ruston
Executive Director
Christian-based substance misuse education. Also
provides resource materials and training for youth
workers.

Ipswich Christian Youth Ministries
6 Great Colman Street, Ipswich,
Suffolk IP4 2AD
Tel 01473 216712
Fax 01473 216712

Mr Nigel Taylor
Team Leader
Schools workers covering primary, junior and
secondary education. Also organises various age-
graded youth events and weekend houseparties;
assists church-based groups, drop-in centre and
training for youth leaders and teachers.

Kidscape
152 Buckingham Palace Road, London
SW1W 9TR

National Council of YMCAs
640 Forest Road, London E17 3DZ

National Council of YMCAs of Ireland
St George's Buildings, 37 High Street,
Belfast BT1 2AB

New Generation Ministries
Severn Ridge, 29 Gloucester Road,
Almondsbury, Bristol BS12 4HH

Mr & Mrs Ray & Nancy Goudie
Directors

Oasis Trust
87 Blackfriars Road, London SE1 8HA
Tel 0171 928 9422
Fax 0171 928 6770
emai 100620.3640@compuserve.com

Revd Steve Chalke
General Director
Started in 1985, Oasis Trust motivates and enables
evangelism, training and social care, in partnership
with local churches in the UK and abroad.

ORGANISATIONS

Oxford Youth Works
Old Mission Hall, 57b St Clements, Oxford
OX4 1AG
Tel 01865 251866
Fax 01865 201005

Mrs Sam Richards
Director & Senior Tutor
Training centre for the practice of Christian relational care as a basis for youth ministry. Runs a number of pioneering projects among unchurched young people.

Pioneer TIE Teams
PO Box 79c, Esher, Surrey KT10 9LP

The Salmon Youth Centre
43 Old Jamaica Road, London SE16 4TE
Tel 0171 237 3788
Fax 0171 252 0285

Mr Jonathan Farnhill
Director
The Salmon Youth Centre in Bermondsey, in association with other agencies, exists to meet the physical, social, intellectual, emotional and spiritual needs of young people, and campaign for their rights.

Scripture Union
207 Queensway, Bletchley, Milton Keynes,
Buckinghamshire MK2 2EB
Tel 01908 856000
Fax 01908 856111
email postmaster@scriptureunion.org.uk

Revd John Simmons
Chair of Council
Makes Jesus known to young people. Works in schools, on holidays, in missions, plus resourcing and training churches in their work with young people, especially in Bible reading.

Scripture Union Northern Ireland
157 Albertbridge Road, Belfast BT5 4PS
Tel 01232 454806
Fax 01232 739758
email 100272.1727@compuserve.com

Revd David Bruce
General Director
Advises on and sells a large range of resources suitable for use in all areas of youth ministry, including a video hire library.

Scripture Union Scotland
9 Canal Street, Glasgow G4 0AB
Tel 0141 332 1162
Fax 0141 332 5925
email 100522.2771@compuserve.com

Revd Colin Sinclair
General Director
By the year 2000 aims to be working with the churches to be reaching everyone of school age in Scotland with the good news of Jesus.

Soapbox Expeditions
14 Cranbrook Terrace, Cranleigh, Surrey
GU6 7ES
Tel 01483 271015
Fax 01483 273872

Revd Steve Flashman
National Director
Communicates the radical edge of the gospel through media, arts, schools, publishing, training workshops, tours and Third World expeditions.

Soul Survivor
37 Quickley Lane, Chorleywood,
Hertfordshire WD3 5AE
Tel 01923 446655
Fax 01923 447007

Mr Mike Pilavachi
Reaches and equips those in their teens and 20s and provides resources for those who want to work with them. Includes conferences, training, festivals, concerts and a youth magazine.

TEAR Fund
100 Church Road, Teddington, Middlesex
TW11 8QE
Tel 0181 943 7779
Fax 0181 943 3594
email pxh@tearfund.dircon.co.uk

Mr Doug Balfour
General Executive Director
Third World relief and development charity dedicated to helping the world's poor. Publishes resource materials to help young people think and act globally and provides opportunities to work with the poor abroad and in the UK.

TEAR Fund Youth Co-ordinators
Ireland:
Clare Henderson
23 University Street, Belfast BT7 1FY
Tel 01232 324940

North & Midlands:
Mark Elder
7 Olympia Street, Burnley, Lancashire
BB10 4EW
Tel 01282 830685

Scotland:
Linsey Matthews
Challenge House, 29 Canal Street,
Glasgow G4 0AD
Tel 0141 332 3621

South & West:
Marvin Rees
c/o Tear Fund, 100 Church Road,
Teddington, Middlesex TW11 8QE
Tel 0181 977 9144

Teen Challenge
52 Penygroes Road, Gorslas, Llanelli,
Dyfed SA14 7LA

TES (The Evangelization Society)
64 Cricklade Road, Gorse Hill, Swindon,
Wiltshire SN2 6AF
Tel 01793 481444
Fax 01793 435237

Mr Ron Spillards
Director
Enables a team of itinerant evangelists to specialise in evangelism throughout the UK. Provides resources to train young people in evangelism.

Time For God
2 Chester House, Pages Lane, Muswell
Hill, London N10 1PR
Tel 0181 883 1504
Fax 0181 365 2471

Mr Roger Taylor
Director
A full-time Christian volunteering scheme for 17-25s. Opportunities available from September and January for 9-12 months in churches, hostels, YMCAs, community centres, schools for disabled, etc.

Universities and Colleges Christian Fellowship of Evangelical Unions (UCCF)
38 De Montfort Street, Leicester LE1 7GP
Tel 0116 255 1700
Fax 0116 255 5672
email uccf@cix.compulink.co.uk

Revd Bob Horn
General Secretary
Supports university and college Christian Unions in their work of student evangelism and Christian training.

Viz-a-Viz
227 Rayleigh Road, Hutton, Brentwood, Essex CM3 1PJ

Wavelength Trust
236 Sebert Road, Forest Gate, London E7 0NP

The Way
CWR , Waverley Abbey House, Waverley Lane, Farnham, Surrey GU9 8EP
Tel 01252 783695
Fax 01252 783847
email 100451.3112@compuserve.com

Mr Sean Grubb
Head of Ministry Operations
Resources youth groups, churches and schools through multi-media Bible teaching events (Insite), Bible reading notes (YPs) and curriculum-based lessons and assemblies in schools.

Wycliffe Youth Team
Wycliffe Bible Translators, Horsleys Green, High Wycombe, Buckinghamshire HP14 3XL
Tel 01494 482521
Fax 01494 483297
email liz.thomson@iccs.sil.org

Miss Liz Thomson
Youth Team Co-ordinator
Uses an interactive approach to introduce the challenge of communicating the Christian faith in different cultures and languages to teenagers and children. Publishes youth group meeting plans on mission.

YMCA Scotland
11 Rutland Street, Edinburgh EH1 2AE

Young Friends General Meeting
Quaker Meeting House, Meeting House Lane, Lancaster, Lancashire LA1 1TX

Young Life
Spring Cottage, Spring Road, Leeds LS6 1AD
Tel 0113 275 3565
Fax 0113 230 4362

Mr Trevor Knight
Director
Co-ordinates branches run for teens and 20s. Publishes youth magazine, resources and runs activity holidays.

Youth For Christ (YFC)
PO Box 5254, Halesowen, Birmingham,
West Midlands B63 3DG
Tel 0121 550 8055
email 100434.3535@compuserve.com

Mr Roy Crowne
National Director

Youth for Christ (YFC) Local Centres:
Aberdeen YFC, 49 Gilcomston Park,
Aberdeen AB1 1PA
Tel 01244 648050

Kate Wells
Director

Ashby YFC, 60 Market Street, Ashby-de-la-
Zouch, Leicestershire LE6 5QF
Tel 01530 560940

Nigel Roberts
Director

Aylesbury Vale YFC, 8 Dane Court,
Aylesbury, Buckinghamshire HP21 8BH
Tel 01296 29838

Graham Arnold
Centre Worker

Bath YFC, St Matthew's Church,
Widcombe Hill, Bath, Avon BA2 6AA
Tel 01225 336055/0421 519435
email 100425.1205@compuserve.com

Nick Shephard
Director

Burntwood YFC, c/o Burntwood Elim
Church, High Street, Chasetown, West
Midlands WS7 8XQ
Tel 01543 683692

Lloyd Cheshire
Director

Burton YFC
54 Uxbridge Street, Burton-on-Trent,
Staffordshire DE14 3JR
Tel 01283 531722

Camberley YFC
33 Salisbury Grove, Camberley, Surrey
GU16 6BP
Tel 01252 876414

Sarah Bolton
Staff Worker

Central Scotland YFC
10-12 Primrose Street, Alloa FK10 1JG
Tel 01259 210808

Eddie Williamson
Director

ORGANISATIONS

Cheltenham YFC
St Paul's Centre, St Paul's Road,
Cheltenham, Gloucestershire
GL50 4EZ
Tel 01242 524408

Richard Passmore
Director

Coventry YFC
Pulse Nightclub, Coventry YFC Studio,
New Buildings, Coventry CV1 5EQ
Tel 01203 550257

Steve Smith
Director

Derby YFC
19 Woodlea Grove, Little Eaton, Derby
DE21 5EN

Liz Morgan
Chairman

Dorking YFC
6 Falkland Road, Dorking, Surrey
Tel 01306 889513

Tim Ward
Secretary

Driffield YFC
31 Thorndale, Wetwang, Driffield,
Yorkshire YO25 9XZ

F. James
Director

Epping Forest YFC
Latchett Church, Latchett Road,
South Woodford, London E18 1DL
Tel 0181 502 9791

Tim Packham
Director

Guernsey YFC
2 Heathfield, Fosse Andre, St Peter Port,
Guernsey
Tel 01481 722755

David Russell
Director

Harrogate & District YFC
49 Dragon Avenue, Harrogate, Yorkshire
HG1 5DS
Tel 01423 507527

Paul Easby
Joint Director

Hemel YFC
43 Ritcroft Close, Hemel Hempstead,
Hertfordshire
Tel 01442 218117

Tony Dussek
Director

Hull YFC
Good News Bookshop,
67 Wright Street, Hull HU2 8JD
Tel 01482 226137

Inverclyde YFC
Gibshill Community Centre, Thomas Muir
Street, Greenock, Inverclyde PA15 2RF
Tel 01475 745645

Inverness YFC
26 Broom Drive, Drummond, Inverness
IV2 4EG

D. Black
Chairman

Kenilworth YFC
2 Spring Lane, Kenilworth, Warwickshire
CV8 2HB
Tel 01926 52117

Gavin Coxhead
Director

Leicester YFC
98 Luther Street, Leicester LE3 0QG
Tel 0116 254 8176

Lincoln YFC
The Rock Diner, 72 Park Street, Lincoln
LN2 5AR
Tel 01522 545397/0378 317970

Newmarket & District YFC
Mulberry House, 31 Market Street,
Fordham, Ely, Cambridgeshire CB7 5LQ
Tel 01638 721339

Jerry Bendall
Director

Norwich YFC
70 Catton Grove Road, Norwich, Norfolk,
NR3 3NT
Tel 01603 415756

Ian Savory
Director

Peterborough YFC
45 Penrith Grove, Peterborough PE4 7FQ
Tel 01733 325873

ORGANISATIONS

Potters Bar YFC   **John Walford**
50 Hill Rise, Potters Bar, Hertfordshire
EN6 2RR
Tel 01707 658396

Preston YFC   **Des Wadsworth**
20 Turpin Green Lane, Leyland, Preston,   *Senior Worker/Schools Worker*
Lancashire PR5 2EA
Tel 01772 629314
Fax 01772 629314

Rugby YFC   **Iain Bruce**
52 Arch Road, Wyken, Coventry,   *Acting Director*
Warwickshire CV2 5AB
Tel 01203 617684

Solent YFC   **Martin Mant**
205 London Road, North End, Portsmouth,   *Director*
Hampshire PO2 9AJ
Tel 01705 610609

South Somerset YFC   **Peter Davies**
c/o Yeovil Community Church, Preston
Chapel, 164 Preston Road, Yeovil,
Somerset BA20 2EQ
Tel 01935 33146

South Trafford YFC
Suite 4, Orchard House, Orchard Place,
Sale , Cheshire M33 7XB
Tel 0161 962 0009/0973 519212
email 100763.713@compuserve.com

Swansea YFC   **Maynard Davies**
41 Porth-Y-Waun, Gowerton, Swansea   *Director*
SA4 3BJ
Tel 01792 872988

Tamworth YFC   **Mark Stafford**
33 Browns Lane, Tamworth, Staffordshire   *Chairman*

Thamesdown YFC
11 Farringdon Road, Swindon, Wiltshire
SN1 5AR
Tel 01793 531810
email 100451.255@compuserve.com

Tyneside YFC   **Phil Glover**
14a Pilgrim Street,   *Director*
Newcastle-upon-Tyne NE1 1BR
Tel 0191 261 0752
Fax 0191 261 0752
email 100546.2013@compuserve.com

Waltham Forest YFC   **Andy Hough**
80 Palmerston Road, Walthamstow,   *Director*
London E17 6PZ
Tel 0181 521 9505

Warrington YFC   **Nigel Lane**
PO Box 323, Warrington, Cheshire   *Director*
Tel 01925 240862/0973 628501
email 100410.616@compuserve.com

Wearside YFC   **Chris Bambrough**
1 Oswald Terrace West, Castletown,   *Director*
Sunderland, Tyne & Wear SR5 3BA
Tel 0191 516 0945
Fax 0191 516 0974

West Cornwall YFC   **Simon Hughes**
Treloquithack, Meadow Bank Road,   *Director*
Falmouth, Cornwall TR11 2ND
Tel 01326 211401

West Dorset YFC   **Simon Bowkett**
11 Church Close, Church Street,   *Director*
Dorchester, Dorset DT1 1JN

ORGANISATIONS

Wirral YFC
PO Box 13, West Kirby, Wirral, Merseyside
L48 8DA
Tel 0151 650 1063

Annamarie Gillett
Schools Worker

Wycombe YFC
Kingfisher House, 109a West Wickham
Road, High Wycombe HP12 3AB
Tel 01494 522777

David Allsop
Director

YFC in London
St Michael's House, 2 Elizabeth Street,
London SW1W 9RB
Tel 0171 730 4113
Fax 0171 730 5113
email 100440.1015@compuserve.com
email 100750.1422@compuserve.com

Jon Baker
Joint Director
Dennis Birch
Area Director

YFC in Scotland
Challenge House, 29 Canal Street,
Glasgow G4 0AD
Tel 0141 332 5606
Fax 0141 332 5608
email 101510.1300@compuserve.com

Eddie Lyle
Area Director

Youth for Christ Northern Ireland
3 Fitzwilliam Street, Belfast BT9 6AW
Tel 01232 332277
Fax 01232 230024
email 100734.3634@compuserve.com

Mr John Duncan
National Director
Direct evangelism and the development and
motivation of young Christians through events, team
ministry, local centres and discipleship.

Youth Ministries International
Christian Centre, Bulkington Road,
Bedworth, Warwickshire CV12 9DG
Tel 01203 643415
Fax 01203 643503

Mr John Smith
General Administrator
Trains youth leaders and church planters in Eastern
Europe, sending teams from the UK to Eastern
Europe. Also receives teams from the United States
into the UK.

Youth With A Mission England
Highfield Oval, Ambrose Lane, Harpenden,
Hertfordshire AL1 1JL
Tel 01582 765481
Fax 01582 768048

Mr Laurence Singlehurst
Director
Supports local churches in training youth leaders to
disciple young people and to equip them for mission
and to reach their generation in culturally relevant
settings.

Youth With A Mission Wales
Orama, High Street, Weston Rhyn,
Oswestry, Shropshire SY10 7RP
Tel 01691 773648
Fax 01691 773648

Mr David Davis
Director
Youth work consultancy, training for part-time youth
leaders, discipleship courses for youth groups. Also
provides youth evangelists for missions.

Youthwork Magazine
37 Elm Road, New Malden, Surrey KT3
3HB
Tel 0181 942 9761
Fax 0181 949 2313
email youthwork@trinity-square.co.uk

Mr John Buckeridge
Executive Editor
Monthly magazine providing ideas, resources and
guidance for youth ministry. Read by over 13,000
Christian youth workers.

YWCA of Great Britain
Clarendon House, 52 Cornmarket Street,
Oxford OX1 3EJ

ORGANISATIONS

RESIDENTIAL CENTRES/
YOUTH HOLIDAYS

Key:
  Address
  Tel/Fax/E-mail

Senior staffworker/post
Description of work
Maximum accommodation number
Seating capacity of largest room
Catering style/options (F/B = Full Board, S/C = Self Catering)
Up to 10 facilities/activites offered

Abernethy Outdoor Centre
Nethybridge, Inverness-shire PH25 3ED
Tel 01479 821279
Fax 01479 821279

Mrs M. Gray
Centre Director
One of four Abernethy Trust Ltd residential centres providing outdoor experiences for people of all ages within a Christian environment.
48+ (Main house), 32 (chalets)
90
Main House F/B, chalets F/B or S/C
Skiing, sailing, wind-surfing, canoeing, rock climbing, indoor heated swimming pool, sports hall, all-weather tennis court, large-screen video projector, assault course, etc.

Pioneer Centre
Action Centres UK Ltd, Cleobury Mortimer, Kidderminster, Worcestershire DY14 8JG
Tel 01299 271217
Fax 01299 270948

Mr R. Robertshaw
Centre Director
-
244
250
F/B
Archery, aerial runway, assault course, abseiling, orienteering, kayaking, raft building, swimming pool, games room, disco/barn dance.

Ardeonaig Outdoor Centre
By Killin, Perthshire FK21 8SY
Tel 01567 820523
Fax 01567 820523

Mr P. Simpson
Centre Manager
One of four Abernethy Trust Ltd residential centres providing outdoor experiences for people of all ages within a Christian environment.
45
65
F/B
Cross-country skiing, kayaking, open canoeing, abseiling, sports hall, games room, fitness trail, field studies classroom.

Ardgour Outdoor Centre

Kilmalieu, Ardgour, Inverness-shire PH33 7AD
Tel 01967 411222
Fax 01967 411222

Mrs J. Mackie
Centre Director
One of four Abernethy Trust Ltd residential centres providing outdoor experiences for people of all ages within a Christian environment.
30
25
F/B
Hill walking, rock climbing, downhill skiing, kayaking, open canoeing, sailing, adventure course, orienteering, archery, four-lane Scalextric.

Arran Outdoor Centre

Shiskine, Isle of Arran KA27 8EW
Tel 01770 860330
Fax 01770 860330

Mr P. Jones
Centre Director
One of four Abernethy Trust Ltd residential centres providing outdoor experiences for people of all ages within a Christian environment.
40
80
F/B
Mountain biking, hill walking, canoeing, sea cruising and fishing, gorge walking, abseiling, adventure course, environmental studies laboratory, games hall.

Assembly of God Scottish Youth Camp

Camp Office, 49 Bridge Street, Musselburgh, East Lothian EH21 6AA
Tel 0131 665 0303

Revd Steve Ritchie
Director
Residential youth camp and weekends for 10-13s and 14+.
130
-
F/B
Skiing, skating, go-karts, swimming, badminton, orienteering, canoeing.

Badenoch Christian Centre

Kincraig, Kingussie, Inverness-shire PH21 1NA
Tel 01540 651373

Revd Bill Ross
Warden
-
36
60
(At or nearby) Hill walking, skiing, mountain biking, orienteering, watersports, pony trekking, skating, swimming, table tennis.

Barnabus Trust

Carroty Wood, Higham Lane, Tonbridge, Kent TN11 9QX
Tel 01732 354690
Fax 01732 360429

Mr Graham Horsnell
Chief Executive
Four holiday camps designed for youth groups; Carroty Wood and Halls Green in Kent, Whithaugh Park in the Scottish borders and Climping Centre in Sussex. For small or larger groups. Camping or lodges, activities, meeting rooms, woodland, self-catering or full board.

RESIDENTIAL CENTRES

Blaithwaite Christian Centre

Blaithwaite House, Wigton, Cumbria
CA7 0AZ
Tel 016973 42319
Fax 016973 42319

Mr David Bowie
Centre Manager
Residential centre situated within easy reach of
northern lakes, Salway coast and Eden valley. Three
separate buildings give flexibility of accommodation
and prices.
111
20
F/B or S/C
Assault courses, archery, children's play area, rifle
range, nature trails, football, volleyball, crazy golf,
BMX track.

Camas Adventure Camp/Iona Community

Bunessan, Isle of Mull PA67 6DX
Tel 01681 700404
Fax 01681 700460

Revd Peter Miller
Abbey Warden
Adventure based residential holidays. Groups live in
an isolated setting. Courses look at how we live as
individuals and groups in an increasingly threatened
environment.
20
30
F/B
Kayaking, raft building, problem solving, a night in a
cave, sea fishing, camping, walking, arts and crafts.

Capernwray Hall

Carnforth, Lancashire LA6 1AG
Tel 01524 733908
Fax 01524 736681

Revd Mark Thomas
Managing Director
Situated at the southern end of the English Lake
District.
250
300
F/B
Indoor heated swimming pool with sauna, tennis
courts, volleyball, basketball, table tennis, 175-acre
parkland and gardens.

CCI UK

PO Box 169, Coventry, West Midlands
CV1 4PW
Tel 01203 559099
Fax 01203 559099

Mr Leigh Belcham
National Co-ordinator
Free venue finding service for youth group
weekends/holidays. Also provides `Key Resource
Sheets' on all aspects of organisation/leadership of
residential events.

Christian Youth Enterprises Sailing Centre

The Gerald Daniel, Chidham, Chichester,
West Sussex PO18 8TE
Tel 01243 573375

Mr Norman Doney
Director
Living on board an ex-Navy Mine Sweeper.
35
50
F/B or S/C
Sailing, kayaking, assault course, raft building,
orienteering, field studies, swimming.

Cornerstone Quest

Gwen Genau, Arenig, Bala,
Gwynedd LL23 7PB
Tel 01678 520735

Mr Tim Jones
Centre Manager
Comfortable, simple accommodation in an old
farmhouse for groups from 8 to 30 people. Optional
outdoor activities.
30
40
S/C or F/B
Rock climbing, mountain walking, gorge walking, raft
building, canoeing, sailing, archery, snooker, table
tennis, orienteering.

Crusaders Holidays

2 Romeland Hill, St Albans, Hertfordshire
AL3 4ET
Tel 01727 855422
Fax 01727 848518

Mr Nigel Hall
Holidays Manager
A range of UK-based Christian holidays for young
people from both within and outside Crusaders.

CYFA Pathfinder Ventures Ltd

CPAS, Athena Drive, Tachbrook Park,
Warwick CV34 6NG
Tel 01926 334242
Fax 01926 337613

Mr Geoff Mason
Head of Ventures
Organises residential activities for young people
aged 9-19, primarily from Explorer, Pathfinder or
CYFA groups. The majority take place during the
summer holidays. Also organises Falcon Camps –
week-long residential activities for 8-17s from inner-
city or disadvantaged backgrounds.

Discovery Cruising

Quiraing, Onich, Fort William, Inverness-
shire PH33 6SB
Tel 01855 821371
Fax 01855 821371

Mr Melville Paton
Skipper
Cruises on Scotland's west coast in modern
certificated yachts in accordance with all regulations
and with fully qualified skippers. Visits to Scottish
islands. Live on board. Christian teaching
programme available.
12
-
F/B

Dorset Christian Activity Centre

20 Iddesleigh Road, Bournemouth,
Dorset BH3 7JR
01202 553855

Mr Michael Hart
Director
Activity courses tailored to youth and adult groups in
self-development, leadership training - includes
teaching and fellowship.
30
40
S/C
Canoeing, caving, climbing, orienteering,
trampolining, power boating, water skiing, air rifles,
archery, arts and crafts.

RESIDENTIAL CENTRES

Elim Youth Camp
1 Raynel Mount, Coowridge, Leeds
LS16 6BR
Tel 0113 243 1375

Revd Steve Reilly
Camp Leader
-
600
300
F/B or S/C
Camp site near Bridlington, 100 yards from the
beach. Sports and trips organised daily. Full youth
and adults Bible programme.

The Eton Dorney Centre
The Vicarage, Lake End Road, Dorney,
Windsor, Berkshire SL4 6QS
Tel 01628 662823
Fax 01628 662583

Mr Colin Morton
Warden
Ideal for every youth group.
35
35
F/B
Table tennis, snooker, volleyball, boating.

The Fair Glade Trust
Old School House, Church Lane, Witney,
Oxfordshire OX8 6LA
Tel 01993 703308
Fax 01993 703308

Mr Jonathan Cox
Director
Outdoor activities for youth groups or schools.
-
-
S/C
Canoeing, kayaking, abseiling, archery, sailing,
expeditions.

Fellowship Afloat Trust
The Sail Lofts, Woodrolfe Road,
Tollesbury, Essex CM9 8SE
Tel 01621 868113
Fax 01621 868533

Mr David Hillyer
Director
Residential outdoor activities centre in unique setting
of newly converted light vessel moored in the
Saltmarsh estuary. RYA Sail training, retreats.
36
50
F/B
Dinghy sailing tuition, powerboat training, arts and
crafts, bird watching, environmental studies,
development training.

Frontier Centre
Welford Avenue, Irthlingborough,
Northants NN9 5XA
01933 651718
01933 651893

Mr Victor Allen
Centre Director
-
92
100
-
Abseiling, climbing, kayaking, canoeing, rafting,
orienteering, assault course, archery, initiative
games.

Gaines Christian Youth Centre
Whitbourne, Worcester WR6 5RD
Tel 01886 821212
Fax 01886 821212

Mr Graham Woods
Director
Many on-site activities supervised by trained centre staff. The centre has a proven track record over 33 years.
115
110
F/B
Heated indoor swimming pool, go-karts, mountain bikes, assault course, death slide, kayaking, football, tennis, table tennis, pool tables.

Gloucester Diocesan Camping and Residential Centres
St Mary's Gate, St Mary's Street, Gloucester GL1 2QR
Tel 01452 410022
Fax 01452 308324

Mrs Heather Hodges
Executive Officer
Two residential centres; one camping/adventure centre with tents, marquee, kitchen, shower/toilet block.
60
60
S/C
Rock climbing, abseiling, caving, pony trekking.

Greenhill YMCA
Donard Park, Newcastle, County Down BT33 0GR
Tel 013967 23172
Fax 013967 23172

Mr Tim Hodnett
Centre Director
Site overlooks Dundrum Bay on the slopes of the Mourne Mountains.
48 winter, 122 summer
70
F/B
Canoeing, kayaking, low/high ropes course, aerial runway, orienteering, climbing, abseiling.

Hants & Dorset Christian Youth Camps
16 Darwin Avenue, Christchurch, Dorset BH23 2JB
Tel 01202 475540

Mr Brian Collie
Administrator
Tent accommodation.
110
170
F/B
Swimming, sailing, archery, mountain biking, windsurfing.

Horstead Centre
Rectory Road, Horstead, Norwich NR12 7EP
Tel 01603 737215
Fax 01603 737494

Mrs Val Khambatta
Warden
Young people's residential/activity centre providing the opportunity for spiritual, physical, intellectual and social development within a caring Christian community.
36
30
F/B
Archery, open canoeing, abseiling, rowing, raft building, sailing, rope bridge, climbing.

RESIDENTIAL CENTRES

Hothorpe Hall
Theddingworth, Lutterworth,
Leicestershire LE17 6QX
Tel 01858 880257
Fax 01858 880979

Mr Brian Dunning
Director
Residential conference centre for 10-150 people with
good facilities for the disabled.
150
150
F/B
Football, badminton, volleyball, basketball, table
tennis, pool table, games hall, 12 acres of grounds.

Kilravock Granary
Kilravock Castle, Croy,
Inverness IV1 2PJ
Tel 01667 493258
Fax 01667 493258

Mr Graham Ford
Centre Manager
Converted granary with bunk accommodation that
sleeps 40. Set in extensive woodland estate, off the
beaten track.
40
40
S/C
Nature trails, snooker, table tennis, tennis, volleyball,
croquet, field study.

King's Park Conference Centre
King's Park Road, Moulton Park,
Northampton NN3 6LL
Tel 01604 499699
Fax 01604 499656

Mr Derek Redpath
Centre Director
Residential conference centre with 50 twin-bedded
en-suite rooms and conference facilities for up to
200. Indoor sports arena offers a wide variety of
sports/activities.
100
200
Five-a-side football, roller skating, badminton,
squash, archery, unihoc, volleyball, netball,
trampolining, fencing.

Kingsway Adventure Centre
Alston Road, Middleton-in-Teesdale,
County Durham DL12 OUU
Tel 01833 640881
Fax 01833 640155
email 100672.463@compuserve.com

Mr Adam Hearn
Principal
Family-run Christian activity centre in the heart of the
Pennines.
42
150
F/B or S/C
Climbing, caving, canoeing, rafting, gorge walking,
ropes course, archery, air rifles, orienteering.

Letton Hall Trust
Shipdham, Thetford, Norfolk IP25 7SA
Tel 01362 820717
Fax 01362 820877

Mr Peter Carroll
Director
Residential conference, houseparty and activities
centre providing affordable accommodation in the
heart of rural Norfolk.
150
150
F/B or S/C
Go-karting, games room, cycling, adventure trail,
four-track Scalextric.

Living Waters
Dolwen, Abergele, Clwyd LL22 8NY
Tel 01492 680256
Fax 01492 680267

Mr David Philpott
Director
Youth and church residential facilities.
180
150
F/B
Swimming pool, games rooms, tennis, football,
woodland trails.

Mansfield Outdoor Centre
Manor Road, Lamborne End, Essex
RM4 1NB
Tel 0181 500 3047
Fax 0181 559 8481

Mr Graham Head
Manager
This charity prioritises inner-city groups and those in
need (eg special needs, those at risk), offering
outdoor activities for personal development.
40
40
S/C
Open canoeing, sailing, kayaking, archery, ropes
course, night exercise, wheelchair abseil, problem
solving exercise, farm.

Min-Y-Don Christian Adventure Centre
Arthog, Gwynedd LL39 1BZ
Tel 01341 250433/250487

Mr Antony Boot
Director
Adventure holidays for families, youth groups and
school groups.
50
75
F/B
Canoeing, climbing, abseiling, archery, orienteering,
swimming, fishing, tennis, table tennis, pool table.

Moorlands College
Sopley, Christchurch, Dorset BH23 7AT
Tel 01425 672369

Dr Derek Copley
Principal
-
94
450
Volleyball, netball, unihoc, table tennis, snooker,
short tennis.

Morning Star Trust
No 7 Covered Slip, Chatham Historic
Dockyard, Chatham, Kent ME4 4TE
Tel 01634 403890
Fax 01634 403890

Miss Jane Girlow
Administrator
Provides young people with the opportunity to sail as
the crew of a 62-foot ketch. Ideal for team building
and fellowship. No experience necessary.
11
-
F/B
Sailing

PCW Youth Service & Residential Centre

Coleg Y Bala, Ffrydan Road, Bala, Gwynedd LL23 7RY
Tel 01678 520565
Fax 01678 520565

Revd Bryn Williams
Director
Proclaims the gospel to children and young people throughout Wales and helps develop the whole person mentally, physically and spiritually in a Christian atmosphere.
50
60
F/B
Mountain bikes, assault course, gorge walking, canoeing, swimming, snooker, pool table, table tennis, five-a-side football.

The Quinta

Quinta Hall, Weston Rhyn, Oswestry, Shropshire SY10 7LR
Tel 01691 773696
Fax 01691 774687

Mr Peter Bevington
Centre Manager
Recently completed internal re-building programme on a youth oriented Severn Lodge complex for groups of 10 or more.
240
450
F/B or S/C
Outdoor swimming pool, floodlit hard court games area, football, basketball, volleyball, table tennis, sports hall, putting, fishing.

St Mark's College

Audley End, Saffron Walden, Essex
Tel 01799 522006
Fax 01799 520326

Revd Brenda Wallace
Warden
A residential centre for youth work and youth leader training for churches, schools and uniformed organisations. Beautiful medieval building in rural surroundings.
40
100
F/B
Archery, rifle shooting, brass rubbing, games field, barn for indoor games, table tennis, own chapel, activity packs, initiative games.

St George's Christian Outdoor Centre

St George's House, Georgeham, Devon EX33 1JN
Tel 01271 890755

Mr Martin Larington
Manager
46
46
S/C
Canoeing, rock climbing, abseiling, surfing, topper sailing, mountain biking, horse riding, orienteering.

The Salvation Army

Territorial Youth Department, William Booth Memorial College, Denmark Hill, London SE5 8BQ
Tel 0171 738 5533
Fax 0171 738 6091

Major Ray Bates
Territorial Youth Secretary
Facilities situated at The Salvation Army Youth & Recreation Centre at Sunbury-on-Thames.
120
150
S/C
Swimming pool, orienteering, field sports, table tennis, pool, snooker.

Scripture Union Holidays
207-209 Queensway, Bletchley,
Buckinghamshire MK2 2EB
Tel 01908 856000
Fax 01908 856111
email debbieh@scriptureunion.org.uk

Wide range of activity holidays throughout the UK
and Europe. Choose from over 100, involving more
than 5,000 young people 8-19s, and some families.
Including sports, outdoor pursuits, computing, music,
drama, Bible teaching.

Scripture Union Scotland
9 Canal Street, Glasgow G4 0AB
Tel 0141 332 1162
Fax 0141 332 5925
email 100522.2771@compuserve.com

Revd Colin Sinclair
General Director
40
100
F/B or S/C
Outdoor pursuits, games hall.

Tynddol Challenge Centre
Cwmystwyth, Aberystwyth SY23 4AG
Tel 01974 282618

Mr Robin Morris
Director
Adventure courses for church youth groups, Christian
schools and families. Fully qualified Christian staff.
30
30
F/B
Abseiling, rock climbing, wayfaring, canoeing,
kayaking, expeditions, bivouacking, discipleship
training.

YMCA Otterburn Hall
Otterburn, Northumberland NE19 1HE
Tel 01830 520663
Fax 01830 520491

Mr Chris Jones
Director
Residential centre in Northumberland national park
with conference and training facilities.
140
150
F/B
Tennis court, orienteering, climbing, abseiling,
archery, squash, putting, croquet, argo-riding.

YMCA National Centre
Lakeside, Ulverston, Cumbria LA12 8BD
Tel 015395 31758
Fax 015395 30015

Mr Jim Dobson
Director
Outdoor education and training courses for young
people using a wide range of water and mountain
based activities in a purpose-built environment.
350
180
F/B or S/C
Climbing, abseiling, orienteering, obstacle course,
aerial runway, archery, rafting, Canadian canoe,
sailing, kayaking, initiative/problem solving.

RESIDENTIAL CENTRES

YMCA Scotland
11 Rutland Street, Edinburgh EH1 2AC
Tel 0131 228 1464
Fax 0131 228 5462

Dr John Knox
National General Secretary
120
80
F/B
Mountains, lakes, ecological estates, canoeing,
orienteering, camping, expeditions, gorge walking,
various sports.

The Barn Youth Church
107 Stanstead Road, Forest Hill, London
SE23 1HH
Tel 0181 291 4057
Fax 0181 291 6764

Mr Kevin Braund
Church Leader
New Church (Ichthus Christian Fellowship)
Youth congregation aimed at reaching into youth culture. Creating a form of church which is relevant for the younger generation. Generally uses ambient/dance worship, also other forms of meditation, video images, etc.

Bliss
Digby Chambers, Post Office Road,
Bournemouth, Dorset BH1 1BA

Mr Johnny Sertin
New Church (Pioneer)

Cellar Youth Church
Vineyard House Church, Sandford Orleigh
House, Off Exeter Road, Newton Abbott,
Devon TQ12
Tel 01626 335242
Fax 01626 335242

Mr Daniel Stivey
Youth Leader
Independent Charismatic
Youth church meets on Saturdays, with midweek 'Youth Alpha'.

Crossroads Church (The Deep End)
127 Woodhorn Road, Ashington,
Northumberland NE63 9EU
Tel 01670 523864
Fax 01670 523864

Pastor Dave Merritt
Independent Charismatic
Alternative worship/evangelistic event with ambient/dance style music, computer and video images, smoke and interactive teaching.

Eternity
The Vicarage, Church Lane, Warfield,
Bracknell, Berkshire RG42 6EE
Tel 01344 882228

Mr Mark Meardon
Youth Pastor
Church of England
Fortnightly band-led worship service, making use of video images, lighting and banners. Includes testimonies and talks.

Flare
254 Ringwood Road, Ferndown, Dorset
BH22 9AR
Tel 01202 894004

Mr Tony Thornton
Youth Council Team Leader
Church of England
Youth congregation with youth-oriented worship
which avoids embarrassing or excluding non-
Christians.

Generation
Generation Resource Centre,
Ruxley Lane, Epsom, Surrey KT19 0UY
Tel 0181 786 8221
Fax 0181 393 2916

Mr Russ Oliver
Team Leader
New Church (Pioneer)
Runs a number of youth initiatives and youth
events/celebrations.

Holy Disorder
Trinity Cottage, 3 Old Hospital Lane,
Tewkesbury, Gloucestershire GL20 5NQ
Tel 01684 274259

Mr Ian Long
Youth/Pastoral Assistant
Church of England
Monthly youth-friendly youth service.

Heart & Soul
107 Stanstead Road, Forest Hill,
London SE23 1HH
Tel 0181 291 4057
Fax 0181 291 6764

Mr Roger Forster
Church Leader
New Church (Ichthus Christian Fellowship)
Monthly youth celebration with live band and visuals;
the aim is to create a similar atmosphere to a club
with dance and movement as an essential part of
worship.

Joy
Oxford Youth Works, 57b St Clements,
Oxford OX4 1AG
Tel 01865 251866
Fax 01865 201005

Mrs Sam Richards
Director
Church of England
Monthly alternative worship service, weekly meeting.
Live rock music, pre-recorded dance/ambient music,
loosely based around Anglican communion service,
exploring current themes with meditation and
prayers. Designed to be accessible to unchurched
young people and young adults.

Late Late Service
64 Barrington Drive, Glasgow G4 9ET

Late Night Something
Watnall Road Baptist Church, Watnall
Road, Hucknall, Nottingham NG15 7DL
Tel 0115 968 1189

Mr David Barker
Youth Worker
Baptist/Interdenominational
An experiment in non-sad worship for local youth and
all ages.

Lifetime
146 Bromwich Road, Worcester
WR2 4AS
Tel 01905 424852

Revd Simon Douglas
Co-ordinator
Interdenominational
Alternative worship which includes Anglican,
Methodist, Roman Catholic and Evangelical
traditions, plus an interest in Celtic spirituality.
Features drama, DJ, dance, video, participation
activities, worship band, reflective prayer.

Manna Youth Service
23 Kingsland Road, Broadwater,
Worthing, West Sussex BN14 9EB
Tel 01903 212153

Mr Norman Smith
Parish Youthworker
Church of England
Ambient-style alternative worship led by youth band,
video images with dance and drama.

No Compromise
Elim Christian Centre, Hall Street,
Chelmsford, Essex CM2 0HG
Tel 01245 358855
Fax 01245 496304
email 101522.3004@compuserve.com

Mr Phil Loose
Director
Pentecostal/Interdenominational
Monthly evangelistic alternative worship service for
13+, which regularly attracts 450. Rock, intelligent
lighting, smoke, visuals, teaching.

New Generation Ministries
Severn Ridge, 29 Gloucester Road,
Almondsbury, Bristol BS12 4HH

Rapture
St Peter's Church, Sumner Road, West
Harrow, Middlesex HA1 4BX
0181 4231120

Mr Mike Resch
Youth Worker
Interdenominational
A place for young people to worship and discover
more about God through various forms.

Revive
204 King Lane, Leeds LS17 6AA
Tel 0113 269 3742
Fax 0113 269 0722

Pastor Simon Hall
Baptist
A youth congregation based in a local Baptist church.
Youth led within the `indie' scene. The worship is like
a good gig, visuals like a good REM video, teaching
is participative and practical. Revive offers training in
evangelism, youth worship and church planting.
Music tapes available.

The Rock Communion
236 Serbert Road, Forest Gate,
London E7 0NP
Tel 0181 534 8500

Revd Simon Law
Leader
Church of England
Presents a rock setting of the Anglican ASB Holy
Communion service.

ALTERNATIVE WORSHIP

St Lawrence Youth Church
St Lawrence Church, Westminster Close,
Liverpool L4 1TS
Tel 0151 944 1952

Mr Anthony Clowes
Youth Evangelist
Church of England/Interdenominational
Monthly alternative worship for teens and 20s. Uses
drama, video images, testimony, poetry, worship and
teaching.

Second Eleven
51 Peveril Road, Tibshelf, Alfreton,
Derbyshire DE55 5LR
Tel 01773 872720

Mr Peter South
Youth Ministry Co-ordinator
Church of England
Informal structure with contemporary worship, drama
and participative talks.

Second Wave
Christ Church Office, Christ Church Road,
Winchester, Hampshire SO23 9SR
Tel 01962 854454

Mr Gareth Dickinson
Youth Minister
Church of England
Youth congregation (14-25s) whose primary aims are
evangelism and celebration. Includes prayer, worship
and word ministry.

Soul Survivor
37 Quickley Lane, Chorleywood,
Hertfordshire WD3 5AE
Tel 01923 446655
Fax 01923 447007

Mr Mike Pilavachi
Director
Church of England
Weekly youth congregation features contemporary
band-led worship, focusing on God and letting him
move through intimate worship, teaching and ministry
in the power of the Holy Spirit.

Sublime
Central Hall, St Mary Road, Southampton,
Hampshire SO14 1NF
Tel 01703 237700
Fax 01703 234555

Mr Billy Kennedy
Youth & Student Work Director
New Church
Weekly youth congregation targeting 14-25s in and
around Southampton. Indie-style worship in a
creative environment. Also works into local schools,
colleges and clubs.

Teignbridge Youth Initiative
31 Chantry Close, Teignmouth, Devon
TQ14 8FE
Tel 01626 773000

Mr Dave Llewellyn
Team Leader
Interdenominational
Organise youth events for young people living in the
Teignbridge and surrounding areas.

Ultimate Rhubarb Dreams
The Community Church, The Retreat,
Surbiton, Surrey KT5 8RN
Tel 0181 296 9088
Fax 0181 296 9717

Mr Paul Sanderson
Youth Co-ordinator
New Church (Pioneer)
Provides an opportunity for young people to lead,
speak, dance, worship and receive creative teaching.
Relevant to unchurched youth. Features interactive
discussion, decks, live band, lights, with space for the
prophetic.

Youthbase

327 New Hey Road, East Bowling,
Bradford BD4 7LD
Tel 01274 726952

Mrs Georgina Taylor
Youth Co-ordinator
Church of England
Develops church in youth culture within a cell group
structure. Visual, experimental worship using all the
senses, including dance music and visual images.
Corporate worship with a high level of interaction with
one another, music and God.

Youth Ministries 2000

48 Birch House Road, Chesterton,
Newcastle-under-Lyme ST5 7HB
Tel 01782 866922

Mr Ian Hough
Evangelism Co-ordinator
Interdenominational
Provides the opportunity for young people to come
together to worship God in a charismatic style.

ALTERNATIVE WORSHIP

YOUTH MINISTRY
TRAINING

Key:

Senior Lecturer/Contact
Job title
Denominational affiliation (if given)
Course Title
Course description
Duration
Price

Arran Outdoor Centre
Shiskine, Isle of Arran KA27 8EW
Tel 01770 860333
Fax 01770 860333

Mr Peter Jones
Centre Director
Breakthrough
Outdoor educational experiences as a youth resource.
Weekend/week
£45/£120-170

Barnsbury Youth Project
All Saints' Church, Carnegie Street,
Islington, London N1 0ES
Tel 0171 837 0720

Mr & Mrs Matt & Gemma Brown
Youth Project Leaders
Year In Barnsbury
Church of England
Practical 'hands-on' youth work training, including evangelism and discipleship among local young people.
10 months
£1,500 includes pocket money, living expenses and accommodation.

Birmingham Bible Institute
5 Pakenham Road, Edgbaston,
Birmingham B15 2NN
Tel 0121 440 4016

Revd Dr Richard Massey
Principal

Brainstormers
87 Blackfriars Road, London SE1 8HA
Tel 0171 928 6538

Miss Tina Vygas
Administrator
Brainstormers Weekend Conference
£59.50 plus accommodation
Provides youth ministry training weekend and day conferences. Organised jointly by Oasis Trust, Youthwork magazine and Youth for Christ, the November weekend (Friday evening to Sunday afternoon) conferences in Blackpool and Eastbourne annually attract over 1,300 youth workers for training, encouragement, worship, resources and ideas.

Church Youth Fellowships Association (CYFA)
Athena Drive, Tachbrook Park, Warwick
CV34 6NG
Tel 01926 334242
Fax 01926 337613

Revd Steve Tilley
Head of CYFA
Church of England
Bible-based resources, training and events for 14-18s and their leaders. Training in individual churches, regionally and at national events.

Cliff College
Calver , Sheffield S30 1XG
Tel 01246 582321
Fax 01246 583739

Revd Howard Mellor
Principal
Methodist
Schools Workers Course
5 days
£70
Training and support for youth workers engaged in schools and evangelistic ministries.

Crusaders
2 Romeland Hill, St Albans, Hertfordshire
AL3 4ET
Tel 01727 855422
Fax 01727 848518

Dr Alan Kerbey
National Director
National network of youth groups for outreach to unchurched young people age 4-18. Supported by teaching materials, leadership training, holidays, events and full-time area development workers.

(Northern Ireland) Crusaders
178 Cavehill Road, Belfast BT15 5EX
Tel 01232 712908
email 100760.3275@compuserve.com

Mr Hugh McCullough
N.I. Committee Member
In Focus/Into battle/Basic Training I & II/Into Action
A wide variety of training courses available from weekends to two years in length.

Regents Park Theological College
London Road, Nantwich, Cheshire
CW5 6LW
Tel 01270 610800
Fax 01270 610013

Revd John Smyth
Principal
Elim Pentecostal

Ekklesia Youth Project
PO Box 1041, Sheffield S10 3YA
Tel 0114 230 1928
Fax 0114 230 6568

Mr David Fenton
-
Ekklesia Youth Project
One year
A training course in youth ministry based on the local church.

Frontier Youth Trust
70-74 City Road, London EC1Y 2BJ
Tel 0171 336 7744

Mr Michael Eastman
Secretary & Development Officer
Supports, resources and trains those working with and on behalf of disadvantaged young people.

TRAINING

Hope UK
25f Copperfield Street, London SE1 0EN
Tel 0171 928 0848
Fax 0171 401 3477

Mr George Ruston
Executive Director
Christian-based substance misuse education. Also
provides resource materials and training for youth
workers.

Ichthus Christian Fellowship
107 Stanstead Road, Forest Hill, London
SE23 1HH
Tel 0181 291 4057
Fax 0181 291 6764

Mrs Sue Mitchell
Church Leader
New Church
Youthwork Course
One year
A course for 17-22s in training for church leadership
primarily among young people. Involves evangelism,
discipleship, schools work, etc.

London Bible College
Green Lane, Northwood, Middlesex HA6
2UW
Tel 01923 826061

Revd Dr Derek Tidball
Principal

Moorlands College
Sopley , Christchurch, Dorset BH23 7AT
Tel 01425 672369

Dr D. Copley
Principal
Applied Theology in Youth & Community Work
1-3 years
From £2,400 pa
A Christian training centre equipping people to work
for God. Courses include a one-year certificate in
Youthwork, two-year diploma in Youth & Children's
Work, BA or DipHE in Applied Theology.

New Frontiers International
Woodside Christian Centre, Dover
Crescent, Bedford MK41 8QH
Tel 01234 272022
Fax 01234 350544

Mrs Stephanie Hedley
Administrator
New Church
NFI Frontier Year Project
One year
£1,375 plus accommodation
Provides basic theology alongside practical
experience in a church-based project which involves
a range of aspects of serving, outreach and
developing people skills.

Oasis Trust
87 Blackfriars Road, London SE1 8HA
Tel 0171 928 9422
Fax 0171 928 6770
email 100620.3640@compuserve.com

Mr Mark Vernon
-
Oasis Youth Ministry Course
Two years
£2,900 pa approx
Youth ministry training which includes a church
placement. Validated by the University of Wales.

Oxford Youth Works
Old Mission Hall, 57b St Clements,
Oxford OX4 1AG
Tel 01865 251866
Fax 01865 201005

Mrs Sam Richards
Director & Senior Tutor
Diploma in Youth Ministry
9 months full-time study
£4,200 (includes accommodation)
Training centre for the practice of Christian relational care as a basis for youth ministry. Also runs a number of pioneering projects among unchurched young people.

The Pais Project
Sharon Church, Brendon Avenue,
Moston, Manchester M40 9DN
Tel 0161 682 4646

Revd Paul Gibbs
National Director
Schools & Youth Evangelism Course
One year
£nil
Covers all aspects of schools and youth evangelism, including some Bible/theology study, with a practical emphasis.

Scripture Union
207 Queensway, Bletchley, Milton Keynes,
Buckinghamshire MK2 2EB
Tel 01908 856000
Fax 01908 856111
email postmaster@scriptureunion.org.uk

Revd John Simmons
Chair of Council
School/Advanced School for Schools Workers
5 days
£175
Training for churches and full-time schools/youth workers in schools ministry.

Soul Survivor
37 Quickley Lane, Chorleywood,
Hertfordshire WD3 5AE
Tel 01923 446655
Fax 01923 447007

Mr Mike Pilavachi
Director
Church of England
Body Builders
6 months
Resources and training for those who work among teens and 20s.

Spring Harvest
14 Horsted Square, Uckfield,
East Sussex TN22 1QL
Tel 01825 769111
Fax 01825 769141
email youth@springh.org.uk

Mr Alan Johnson
Executive Director
Youth leadership training, including seminars, advice and practical experience in leading small groups within the youth programme of Spring Harvest.

Sublime
Central Hall, St Mary Street,
Southampton SO14 1NF
Tel 01703 237700
Fax 01703 234555

Mr Billy Kennedy
New Church
Year of Training
One year
£800
Training links to a weekly youth congregation targeting 14-25s in and around Southampton, working in local schools, colleges and clubs.

TRAINING

Viz-a-Viz
227 Rayleigh Road, Hutton, Brentwood,
Essex CM13 1PJ
Tel 01277 215222
Fax 01277 215222

Revd Dennis Pethers
Director
Advanced Volunteers Course
11 months
£3,000
Evangelism training and presentation, working in
partnership with colleges, universities and churches
to present the gospel in relevant ways to young
people today.

Youth Equip
c/o 24 Olton Road, Shirley, Solihull, West
Midlands B90 3NE
Tel 0121 744 3057
Fax 0121 744 2829

Mr Pall Singh
Youth Evangelist
New Church
Youth Equip
12 sessions + w/e away
£60
Training for youth workers, plans to develop an 'Asian
Youth Equip' course.

Youth For Christ (YFC)
PO Box 5254, Halesowen, Birmingham,
West Midlands B63 3DG
Tel 0121 550 8055
email 100434.3535@compuserve.com

Mr Roy Crowne
National Director

Youth With A Mission England
Highfield Oval, Ambrose Lane, Harpenden,
Hertfordshire AL1 1JL

Ms Liz West
Now Youth/Principles in Child & Youth Ministry
Four weekends/12 weeks residential
£120/£600
Supports local churches in training youth leaders to
disciple young people and to equip them for mission
and to reach their generation in culturally relevant
settings.

Youth With A Mission Wales
Orama, High Street, Weston Rhyn,
Oswestry, Shropshire SY10 7RP
Tel 01691 773648
Fax 01691 773648

Mr Martin Abel
Team Leader
Principles in Child & Youth Ministry
3 months + outreach
£780 plus accommodation
Child and youth ministry team training and equipping
people to work with 5-25s through seminars,
resources and courses.

USEFUL

ADDRESSES

African Caribbean Evangelical Alliance
Whitefield House, 186 Kennington Park Road, London SE11 4BT
Tel 0171 735 7373

Alliance Music
PO Box 410, Aylesbury, Buckinghamshire
Tel 01844 292022
Fax 01844 290880

Alpha Course
Holy Trinity Church, Brompton Road, London SW7 1JA
Tel 0171 581 8255

Association of Christian Counsellors
173a Wokingham Road, Reading, Berkshire RG6 1LT
Tel 01734 662207

Bible in Life
Lottbridge Drove, Eastbourne, East Sussex BN23 6NT
Tel 01323 417394

Bible Society
Stonehill Green, Westlea, Swindon, Wiltshire SN5 7DG
Tel 01793 418100

British Red Cross Society
9 Grosvenor Crescent, London SW1X 7EJ
Tel 0171 235 5454
Fax 0171 245 6315

CARE (Christian Action Research and Education)
53 Romney Street, London SW1P 3RF
Tel 0171 233 0455

Christian Aid
35 Lower Marsh, London SE1 7RT
Tel 0171 620 444
Fax 0171 620 0719
email caid@gn.apc.org

Christian Enquiry Agency
Inter-Church House, 35 Lower Marsh, London SE1 7RL
Tel 0171 620 4444

Christian Initiative on Teenage Sexuality
136 Newport Road, Cardiff CP2 1DJ
Tel 01222 494431
Fax 01222 497807

Christian Focus Publications
Geanies House, Fearn, Tain, Ross-shire IV20 1TW
Tel 01862 871541

Church House Publishing
Church House, Great Smith Street, London SW1P 3NZ
Tel 0171 222 9011
Fax 0171 799 2714

Cross Rhythms
PO Box 183, Plymouth PL3 4YN
Tel 01752 225623
Fax 01752 673441

CTVC
Hillside Studios, Merry Hill Road, Bushey, Watford WD2 1DR
Tel 0181 950 4426

CVG Television
First House, 1 Sutton Street, Birmingham
B1 1PE
Tel 0121 622 1337
Fax 0121 622 3080

Duke of Edinburgh's Award Scheme
Gulliver House, Madeira Walk, Windsor,
Berkshire
Tel 01753 810753

Eating Disorders Association
Sackville Place, 44-48 Magdalen Street,
Norwich NR3 1JE
Tel 01603 621414

Evangelical Alliance UK
Whitfield House, 186 Kennington Park
Road, London SE11 4BT
Tel 0171 582 0228
Fax 0171 582 6221

Friends of the Earth
26-28 Underwood Street, London N1 7JQ
Tel 0171 490 1555

Greenbelt Festivals
St Luke's Church, Hillmartin Road,
London N7 9JE
Tel 0171 700 6585

Greenpeace
Cannonbury Villas, London N1 2PN
Fax 0171 354 5100

Harper Collins (Religious)
77 Fulham Palace Road, Hammersmith,
London W6 8JB
Tel 0181 741 7070

Health Education Authority
Hamilton House, Mabledon Place,
London WC1H 9TX
Tel 0171 383 3833

Herald House Ltd
96 Dominion Road, Worthing, West
Sussex BN14 8JP
Tel 01903 821082

Hodder Headline
388 Euston Road, London NW1 3BH
Tel 0171 873 6000

Inter-Varsity Press (IVP)
Norton Street, Nottingham NG7 3HR
Tel 0115 978 1054

Kidscape
152 Buckingham Palace Road, London
SW1W 9TR
Tel 0171 730 3300

Kingsway Publications
Lottbridge Drove, Eastbourne, East
Sussex BN23 6NT
Tel 01323 410930
Tel 01323 411970

Lion Publishing
Peter's Way, Sandy Lane West, Oxford
OX4 5HG
Tel 01865 747550
Fax 01865 747568

London City Mission
175 Tower Bridge Road, London SE1 2AH
Tel 0171 407 7585

March For Jesus
PO Box 39, Sunbury-on-Thames,
Middlesex TW16 6PP
Tel 01932 789681

Monarch Publications
Broadway House, The Broadway,
Crowborough, East Sussex TN6 1HQ
Tel 01892 652364
Fax 01892 663329

Movers & Shakers Artist Promotion & Management
141 Thetford Road, New Malden, Surrey KT3 5DZ
Tel 0181 395 5059

National Bible Society of Scotland
Bible House, 7 Hampton Terrace,
Edinburgh EH12 5XU
Tel 0800 526910
Fax 0131 337 0641

National Youth Agency
17-23 Albion Street, Leicester LE1 6GD
Tel 0116 285 6789
Fax 0116 247 1043

Nelson Word
9 Holdom Avenue, Bletchley, Milton
Keynes, Buckinghamshire MK1 1QR
Tel 01908 648440

Pray For Revival
7 Pakenham Road, Edgbaston,
Birmingham B15 2NN
Tel 0121 440 3105

Send The Light
PO Box 300, Kingstown Broadway,
Carlisle, Cumbria CA3 0QS
Tel 01228 512512

Society for Promoting Christian Knowledge (SPCK)
Holy Trinity Church, Marylebone Road,
London NW1 4DU
Tel 0171 387 5282

Spring Harvest
14 Horstead Square, Uckfield, East
Sussex TN22 1QL
Tel 01825 769111
Fax 01825 769141
email youth@springh.org.uk

Standing Conference on Drug Abuse (SCoDA)
1-4 Hatton Place, Off Hatton Garden,
London EC1N 8ND
Tel 0171 430 2341

The Advisory Council on Alcohol and Drug Education (TACADE)
1 Hulme Place, The Crescent, Salford,
Lancashire M5 4QA
Tel 0161 745 8925

Tear Fund
100 Church Road, Teddington, Middlesex
TW11 8QE
Tel 0181 943 7779
Fax 0181 943 3594
email pxh@tearfund.dircon.co.uk

The Evangelization Society (TES)
64 Cricklade Road, Gorse Hill, Swindon,
Wiltshire SN2 6AF
Tel 01793 481444
Fax 01793 435237

Trinity Square Ltd
37 Elm Road, New Malden, Surrey KT3
3HB
Tel 0181 942 9761
Fax 0181 949 2313
email youthwork@trinity-square.co.uk

World Vision
599 Avebury Boulevard, Milton Keynes
MK9 3PG
Tel 01908 841000
Fax 01908 841021
email 100604.2500@compuserve.com

Young Men's Christian Association (YMCA)
640 Forest Road, London E17 3DZ
Tel 0181 520 5599

**Young Women's Christian
Association (YWCA)**
Clarendon House, 52 Cornmarket Street,
Oxford OX1 3EJ
Tel 01865 726110

YOUTH MINISTRY
RESOURCES

The number and variety of resources available for use in youth ministry is large and growing still further each year. This selection of resources is an attempt to choose the best and most widely used books and curricula. However, I recommend that you visit a Christian bookstore which has a good selection of youth ministry resources and browse through for yourself. You could also write to the main publishers and suppliers (see the directory listing of useful addresses) and ask them to send you their latest catalogue - explain that you are particularly on the lookout for youth ministry resources - then stand back and wait for your postbox to bulge!

Ideas, games, discussion starters

Big Ideas for Small Youth Groups by Patrick Angier & Nick Aiken (Marshal Pickering)
A good selection of both indoor and outdoor games, group builders, socials and meeting outlines for use in a small group.

Creative Ideas for Youth Evangelism by Nick Aiken (Marshall Pickering)
A good range of excellent ideas and meeting plans to inform, enthuse and train young people for evangelism.

Creative Outdoor Work with Young People by Alan Smith (Russell House)
Although not a specifically Christian book, it contains a range of good ideas which will bring the countryside to life and involve young people in creative, thought-provoking games and projects.

Creative Programming Ideas for Junior High Ministry by Steve Dickie & Darrell Pearson (Zondervan)
Principles on programme planning, plus lots of ideas for use with 11-14s in missions, Sunday school, sports, retreats, discipling, etc.

Crowdbreakers by Bob Moffett (Marshall Pickering)
An all-time classic games book with a helpful introductory section on the use and abuse of games.

Drive the Point Home by Graham Twelftree (Monarch)
Contains 200 stories which would make good epilogue talks or sermon illustrations.

Faithbuilders by Patrick Angier (Marshall Pickering)
Stuffed full with a wide range of meeting plans and ideas.

Far Out Ideas for Youth Groups by Wayne Rice & Mike Yaconelli (Zondervan/Youth Specialities)
Several of these wacky games and skits need to be Anglicised to work this side of the pond!

Games Without Frontiers by Pip Wilson (Scripture Union)
A wide range of icebreakers, including some very messy crowdbreakers, plus poems and meeting-length activities. This collection is a classic.

Great Ideas for Small Youth Groups by Wayne Rice (Zondervan/Youth Specialties)
This mix of quiet games, icebreakers, games for use in a small room, special events, outdoor games and social ideas is designed to work well with low numbers.

Great Retreats for Youth Groups by Chris Cannon (Zondervan)
Contains twelve complete youth retreats plus a leaders' training weekend. Also includes a 'What to bring' checklist.

Junior Youthbuilders by Patrick Angier (Marshall Pickering)
Statistics and facts about younger teens, plus an excellent range of session ideas including socials, projects, quizzes, worksheets, games and outdoor activities.

Know Ideas! Serious Fun for Youth Groups by Phil Moon (CPAS)
Whole session plans and a creative range of ideas with leader's instructions and preparation.

More Great Ideas for Secondary Classroom Assemblies by Janet King (Monarch)
Contains 52 classroom assembly outlines based on a theme of a broadly or specifically Christian nature.

Much Ado About Something by Andrew Smith (CPAS)
Simple, short storylines designed for 11-14s to perform. With 42 to choose from, plus helpful directors' tips, this is a useful resource for performance drama or discussion starters.

Music Worth Talking About by Tim & Patty Atkins (Baker)
One hundred discussion starters with topic and Scripture indexes are applied to a range of songs from the 70s/80s from Guns 'n' Roses to Amy Grant.

The New Youth Games Book by Alan Dearling & Howard Armstrong (Russell House Publishing)
A useful introduction on the use and purpose of games leads into a wide variety of ice breakers, relationship building games and most things in between.

Play It! by Wayne Rice & Mike Yaconelli (Zondervan)
This collection of over 400 games ideas is packed with a wide range of ideas which makes it a must-have games book.

Play It Again! by Wayne Rice & Mike Yaconelli (Zondervan)
An excellent range of indoor and outdoor games, which includes a helpful introduction on choosing the right games for your situation.

Prayer Services for Young Adolescents by Gwen Costello (Twenty Third Publications)
Don't be put off by the title. This easy-to-use book includes a wide range of themes that your young people will be able to use in a worship context.

Quick Crowdbreakers & Games for Youth Groups by various authors (Group)
A good range of games and icebreakers.

Quicksilver by Karl Rohnke & Steve Butler (Russell House Publishing)
Contains adventure games, initiative problems, trust building games and icebreakers.

Quick Skits & Discussion Starters by Chuck Bolte & Paul McClusker (Group)
Contains eighteen short dialogues and monologues on various topics, each backed up by discussion questions and Bible references.

Spectacular Stinking Rolling Magazine Book by Pip Wilson (Marshall Pickering)
Pip's amazing Greenbelt Festival show in paperback. Includes interaction games, icebreakers, discussion starters and of course Pip's trademark – spectacularly messy crowdbreakers.

Super Ideas for Youth Groups by Mike Yaconelli & Wayne Rice (Zondervan)
More wacky games from our American cousins.

Tension Getters by Mike Yaconelli & David Lynn (Bible Society)
An excellent selection of discussion starters.

The New Youth Games Book by Alan Dearling & Howard Armstrong (Russell House Publishing)
A wide variety of games from icebreakers to more heavy relational games for established groups. Also includes a couple of games inappropriate for use with a Christian group.

Theme Games by Lesley Pinchbeck (Scripture Union)
Vintage playground and party games adapted and linked with one of 200 themes for use with pre-teens.

Youthwork Ideas! by John Buckeridge (Kingsway)
A wide selection of games and crowdbreakers, including chapters on games/activities for Christmas, Easter and Hallowe'en, plus tips on collecting and adapting your own ideas.

Young People and the Bible by Phil Moon (Marshall Pickering)
A mix of methodology and Bible-based ideas for use in a church youth group.

10-Minute Devotions for Youth Groups by JB. Collingsworth (Group)
A collection of 52 ideas for rapid-fire talks - sketches, games, basic science tricks and physical stunts included.

---

20 More Teen Prayer Services by S Kevin Rogan (Twenty Third Publications)
Prayers, readings and guided meditations, but many of the sessions require a lot of materials and planning.

---

52 Ideas for Secondary Classroom Assemblies by Janet King (Monarch)
A wide range of topical themes which can be adapted for use in a youth group/club.

---

101 Dynamic Ideas for Your Youth Group by Andy Back (Word)
A range of familiar and some new games ideas.

Curriculum and Meeting Plan Series

Creative Bible Lessons on the Life of Christ by Doug Fields (Zondervan)
The twelve meeting plans present different characteristics of Jesus, eg healer, confronter, hero, shepherd. Clear presentation and reproducible worksheets, but lots of American cultural references.

CPAS/CYFA Meeting Plan Series by various authors (CPAS)
A dozen A4 format meeting session books often with reproducible worksheets for use with 14+. Most books contain ten meeting plans and include games, Bible study, quizzes, worksheet and comprehensive leaders' notes. Titles include: All Together Forever (10 meetings on Ephesians), Harping On (Psalms), Just About Coping, Powered Up (Acts), Pressure Points (big issues), Rave On (worship) Repeat Prescription (Ten commandments), You'd Better Believe It (doctrine). Produced by CPAS, affiliated to the Anglican Church, but usable across the denominations.

Custom Curriculum by various authors (David C Cook)
A large number of titles in this range of meeting books is available in the UK aimed at 11-14s, or 15+. Their distinctive feature is the customising options the American publishers provide alongside the standard meeting outline. Each of the five meeting

sessions in each book offers fourteen options to tweak or add to the main content so it applies better to your particular group. Options include large group, small group, know it alls, unchurched, mostly girls, mostly lads, urban, media-friendly, etc. The content is creative and well written by some of America's best youth ministry writers. However with only five meeting plans in each book, the cover price is steep.

The Discovery Wheel by Gillian Ambrose, Andrew Gear, David Green (Church House Publishing)
The 48 topics covered would work best as part of a series of confirmation classes with under 16s. Subjects fall into five categories: Me and God, Me and others, Me and society, Me and my feelings, Me and my world.

Fun Old Testament Bible Studies by Mike Gillespie (Group)
These 32 meeting outlines will help bring the Old Testament to life for younger teens. Each session is divided into dig, discover, experience, grow, covenant and go learning sections. The well-written, easy-to-adapt outlines dip into almost every OT book and include a creative reproducible worksheet.

Get God by the World Wide Message Tribe (Alliance)
A leaders' guide, video and six-part book for each group member make up this excellent resource for introducing young people to the Christian faith. Manchester-based WWMT devised this material to follow up on their schools and concert work. Young people into the rave/dance scene will enjoy the music and appreciate the design and layout of the book. Just because the band is culturally relevant, don't make the mistake of thinking that it is biblically lightweight – this is chunky stuff!

Hands on: Making Confirmation Count (CPAS/National Society)
This discipleship course for 11-16s consists of ten sessions, a video and twenty reproducible sheets, all in a loose-leaf file. The wide range of ideas and creative activities makes this a versatile and useful tool, which is usable beyond the main target use in the Church of England.

Just Looking, Just Starting, Just Growing by John Allan (Bible Society)
Three series of six meeting session plans, plus reproducible worksheets which introduce young people to Christianity who are 'just looking', a new Christians' basics course for those 'just starting', and a further series for those who are 'just growing' in faith. Well-written material which works best with a small group of 15+, with lots of discussion, thinking and reading to do. The leaders' notes are comprehensive, but a significant amount of planning and preparation is required. Recommended for use with young people who can cope with books and group work.

Lightning Bolts Series by Nick Jones (BRF)
A series of ten meeting plans for 11-14s which integrates with ten weeks of daily Bible reading notes for young people. The series includes Struck By God (Mark's Gospel),

Out of This World (God's plan for humankind), Rise up, Wise up (Proverbs), Close Encounters (Luke's Gospel), Getting to Grips with God (basics of the Christian faith).

Serendipity Youth Series by Terry Dunnell, Andrew Graystone, Chris Powell (Scripture Union)
Six A5-format books make up this series of Bible studies designed for use in small groups. Each book contains six meetings which focus on different aspects of being a Christian. The well-written and creative meeting booklets (you need one for each group member) encourage interaction and discussion and are flexible and easy to use.

Talksheets by David Lynn (Zondervan)
A series of five A4-format meeting plan books which focus mainly on discussion and Bible study. Two are aimed at 11-14 (Junior High), two at 15+ (Senior High) and one is for parents so they can see the week-by-week themes and further develop discussion around that subject at home. Each session plan comes with a reproducible worksheet, which although well written is graphically uninspiring. These excellent books need adaption and additional material if they are to work well, but with 50 sessions per book they represent good value for money.

Teach 'Toons by Rick Bundschuh & Tom Finley (Zondervan)
What makes these 50 meeting plans stand out from the rest is the quality and variety of the photocopiable cartoon-style worksheets. An excellent resource for use with 10-14s.

Teenscape - A Personal Safety Programme for Teenagers by Michele Elliott (Health Education Authority)
Abuse, crime, bullying, addiction, gambling and self defence are among the topics covered in these session plans which aim to 'teach young people positive and practical ways for dealing with dangerous situations'.

The Best of Power Pack by Bob Moffett (Scripture Union)
These 42 meeting outlines cover a wide range of topics, originally written for publication in Buzz magazine over ten years ago. An oldie but a goodie!

With or Without You by Liz West & Elaine Williams (Crusaders)
This A4-format publication contains over 120 pages with eleven units on relationships aimed at teenagers. The units cover self-image, relationships with others and God, sexual pressure, trust and respect, when relationships break down and communication. Includes icebreakers, worksheets, drama and role plays, plus Bible study material.

Whose Life is it Anyway? by Andy Hickford (CPO)
This series of eleven meetings is a beginner's guide to Christianity. Contents include leaders' guide and colourful worksheet notes for either 11-14s or 15+.

Youth Alpha by Kirsty Giddy, Simon Jones (HTB Publications)
This adaptation of the highly popular Alpha course, which has introduced thousands of people to the Christian faith, covers the same topics as the adult version – Jesus, his death, faith, the Bible, Holy Spirit, etc. An 11-14s manual and 15+ version comes in a leaders' manual and a booklet for each group member. A typical session also suggests icebreakers which link into the theme to be explored each week, as well as a Bible study, questions and discussion starters.

Youthwork Ready-to-Use Meeting Guides Volume 1, 2, 3, 4 by John Buckeridge (Kingsway)
Each volume contains ten complete meeting plans which include an icebreaker, discussion starter or role play, Bible study, A4-format reproducible worksheet and talk ideas. Volume 1: Christian Basics is an introductory course on Christianity for use with unchurched or churched youngsters. Volume 2: Lifestyle looks at major issues including independence, sex and anger. Volume 3: Culture includes media influences, alcohol, drugs, music and adverts. Volume 4: Belief considers doctrinal issues including truth, resurrection, suffering and the second coming. Volume 5 (relationships) and Volume 6 (evangelism) are due out in 1997.

Yoyo Vols 1, 2, 3, 4 by Peter Graystone, Paul Sharpe and Pippa Turner (Scripture Union)
Each meeting plan features a three-part session consisting of discussion starters, Bible studies, activities, talks and games. The meetings emphasise involvement and are well written and, as you would expect from SU, soaked in Scripture.

'How to', theology, pastoral care

A Health Guide for Small Groups by Anton Beamohl (Small Group Resources)
Although primarily aimed at leaders of adult Bible study groups, the youth worker who leads small group discussions or Bible studies will find this practical training manual useful. Several sections could be adapted to form a training unit for your youth work team.

Bereavement by Judith Green (National Youth Agency)
This pack aims to help leaders understand and help those who are bereaved and to raise awareness of bereavement issues to their youth group. Several group exercises are included. Written from a 'secular' work base, so no mention of prayer, healing etc, but a good starting point nevertheless.

The Christian Youth Manual by Steve Chalke (Kingsway)
Brief chapters on a wide range of youth ministry subjects including principles, planning, pastoral problems and projects. This book is a good and highly practical introduction to youth work.

Christian Youth Work by Mark Ashton & Phil Moon (Monarch)
Arguing that good practice comes from good theology, the authors, who are both former heads of CYFA, examine topics such as adolescent conversion and the nature and role of the church, encouraging the reader to think biblically and critically about youth work attitudes and activities.

The Church and Youth Ministry edited by Pete Ward (Lynx)
There is youth ministry theology and theory to give even the deepest thinker plenty to chew over, provided by nine practitioners writing on aspects of church-based youth work. Highlights include John Allan on the organisation of youth ministries in the local church, Pete Ward on finding the right ecclesial context for youth work, and Simon Hall on youth ministry body language.

Connecting by Paul D. Stanley & J. Robert Clinton (NavPress)
The book to read if you want to understand what mentoring is and how it works. The American authors outline the many different styles of mentoring, ranging from the intense spiritual discipling model to an occasional sponsor-type of career guidance. An intensely practical book born out of experience and research.

Dangerous Obsessions by Andrew Boyd (Marshall Pickering)
From the results of a survey among 500 Year 10 students which showed that occult 'dabbling' is widespread, the author uses case studies, media reports and his own knowledge and experience to build an unpleasant but faithful picture of the problem.

The Discovery Flatpack by various authors (Agape Ministries)
A combination of books, video and tracts on the theory and practice of schools ministry. It includes lesson plans, assembly sketches and discussion starters aimed at secondary school ages.

Get Away by Arlo Reichter (Bible Society)
This is the definitive book on residential youth work. A practical guide on taking your group away for a weekend or longer this book includes ready-made retreat programmes as well as 'how tos' on planning, budgeting, and other potential organisational nightmares!

Gospel Exploded by Bob Mayo (Triangle)
The true story of a Christian youth ministry to unchurched young people in inner London. This book provides challenging insights into the impact the gospel can make on alienated young people in the 1990s. It also highlights some creative methods and some of the pitfalls of costly relational youth work.

In the Evangelical Way by Leslie Francis & David Lankshear (National Society)
This booklet is packed with statistics and analysis on children and young people contacted by evangelical Anglican parishes. An exhaustive survey which deserves

careful study. A companion volume, *In the Catholic Way*, makes a similar analysis of Anglo-Catholic parishes.

Introduction to Youth Ministry by John M. Dettoni (Zondervan)
An important and scholarly book divided into three main sections: foundations for youth ministry, balanced elements of a youth programme, additional programme components. Probably the best and most comprehensive introductory book of its kind from the United States. The chapters on a philosophy of youth work and evaluating your youth work are outstanding.

Fast Moving Currents in Youth Ministry by various authors (Lynx)
Prompted by a research project of 13,000 young people, 27 leading youth ministry specialists explain the implications of these findings for work with young people. The 53 chapters cover a wide range of topics including young people and the law, youth evangelism, self-destruction, race, self-esteem and Christian lifestyle.

Learning Styles by Marlene LeFever (David C Cook)
So much teaching/communication within Christian ministry is lecture based and targets the analytic learner. This book helps you discover the four main learning styles, what learning style you are and, crucially, how to communicate to those who learn in a different way from you. LeFever, a leading American teacher/trainer provides a ground breaking mix of theory and practice.

Mentoring for Mission by Gunter Krallmann (Jensco/Gem)
Subtitled *A handbook on leadership principles exemplified by Jesus Christ*, this book investigates how Jesus trained the disciples for leadership. Biblical and practical, this book is a 'must read' for youth workers who are serious about discipling young people into a mature faith.

The Ministry of Nurture by Duffy Robbins (Zondervan)
A classic book on the theory and practice of helping young people to develop their faith, keys to effective discipleship, and ways to help young people build a faith that lasts.

Nurturing Young Disciples by John Buckeridge (Marshall Pickering)
Why do so many young people fail to develop and grow as new Christians? How can we learn from and adopt Jesus' style of discipling? What makes young people tick? How can we help churched young people mature into men and women of God? Is mentoring a worthwhile strategy with unchurched converts? These are some of the issues covered in this book which includes guest contributors Paul Borthwick, Tony Campolo and Duffy Robbins.

Outside In by Mike Breen (Scripture Union)
Subtitled *Reaching unchurched young people today*, this book by Anglican vicar Mike Breen was borne out of his ministry in Cambridge and Brixton. His innovative youth

ministry is unpacked in *Outside In* most notably in sections on identifying key people in whom God is working, and nurturing faith in young people. Other chapters include communication, developing a total approach, making contact with young people, worship and pastoral care, and an excellent section on leaders and teams.

Reaching and Keeping Teenagers by Peter Brierley (Monarch)
This much quoted from book contains the statistics and analysis from a 1992 survey of teenagers. It resulted in much heart-searching over the numbers of young people opting out of church.

Relational Youthwork edited by Pete Ward (Lynx)
Originally presented as papers to a conference for youth specialists, seven different youth work practitioners write on perspectives on relationships in youth ministry. These include Bob Mayo on evangelism among pre-Christian young people and Christine Cook on programme and relationships in youth ministry.

Teenage Religion and Values by Professor Leslie J. Francis & William K. Kay (Gracewing)
A survey of over 13,000 13 to 15-year-olds has resulted in this authoritative work detailing what teens worry about, their sexual morality, sense of personal well being, belief in the supernatural, disenchantment with politics, and their view on a wide range of issues such as shoplifting, stealing and smoking cannabis.

Understanding Teenagers by Pete Gilbert (Crossway)
Following his successful *Teenage Survival Kit* and the sequel *Teenage Revival Kit*, this book targets parents, youth leaders and pastors. Gilbert provides a framework to aid understanding on how teens think, react and feel.

Working with Teenagers by Nick Aiken (Marshall Pickering)
An unusual combination of youth ministry theory and practical ideas to take and use within one paperback. Divided into three main sections: The church and young people, Pastoral care, and Successful youth work, this is a useful and very practical handbook.

Worship and Youth Culture by Pete Ward (Marshall Pickering)
An honest and readable account of how a group of young people set up an alternative service for unchurched young people in Oxford. Foundational ideas on culturally relevant yet God-centred worship.

Young People and the Bible by Phil Moon (Marshall Pickering)
The author believes that Bible teaching does not get the emphasis it deserves in most church youth groups - or if it does, the style is deadly boring or lacks understanding. Moon addresses this problem head-on with a mixture of methodology and ideas that makes this book a very useful and important resource.

Youth A Part by various authors (Church House Publishing)
This landmark report presented to the Church of England's General Synod in 1996 covers a wide range of youth ministry issues including youth culture, a theology of youth work, youth spirituality and worship, building relationships, how youth workers can best be recruited, supported and trained, and examples of good practice and new ideas. The main challenge is whether the church will embrace 11 to 25-year-olds – will the young people will be apart or a part of the church?

Youth Culture and the Gospel by Pete Ward (Marshall Pickering)
This practical guide calls on Christians to understand and befriend young people and show them the relevance of Jesus in the 1990s. Although some of the examples are now out of date (the book was first printed in 1992), the principles still apply.

Youth Ministry Nuts & Bolts by Duffy Robbins (Zondervan)
Aimed at full-time youth workers, this book written by one of America's foremost youth ministry specialists is all about the basics of youth work in the local church. It includes good research, real-life experiences, checklists and worksheets that will work well in the British scene.

Youthwork and How to Do It by Pete Ward, Sam Adams & Jude Levermore (Lynx)
This excellent self-tutor book comprises eight units, each with a variety of exercises to complete. It has been written out of the shared experiences the authors have of Oxford Youth Works, with its emphasis on relational work to unchurched youth.

YOUTH WORK

'It encourages you to think strategically and long-term and yet offers "life-savers" when in the short-term you are panicking! I read it, I use it, I recommend it.'

HEATHER BOYD
Harrow Churches Schools
Link Worker

'It's got the lot!'

STEVE MALLON
Church of Scotland
Youth Adviser

DON'T MISS OUT ON A SINGLE COPY - SUBSCRIBE TODAY

...st £22.80* we'll deliver YOUTH**WORK** to your door every month. Complete the simple direct debit form below ...'e'll send you FREE OF CHARGE your choice of YOUTH**WORK** Ready To Use Meeting Guides Volume 1, 3 or 4 ...h £6.99 each).

...lete this form and send to:
...**HWORK**, Freepost, 37 Elm
..., New Malden, Surrey KT3 3BR.

...E..

...RESS..

....

....

...TCODE ....

OPTION ONE

...ld like to subscribe by Direct
... - and get my FREE Ready-To-
...Meeting Guide! Please send me
one): Vol 1 Christian Basics;
...Culture; Vol 4 Belief - £22.80*
...year (12 issues)

...e manager of

_____bank.

...ss (of bank)

_____

...ode _____

Sort Code ☐☐ / ☐☐ / ☐☐
Account No. ☐☐☐☐☐☐☐☐

Name of account holder(s):

_____

_____

I/We authorise you until further notice in writing to charge my / our account with unspecified amounts which Trinity Square Ltd may debit thereto by Direct debit in respect of my / our annual magazine subscription.

Signed _____

Office Use - Originators No.
954471 Reference No._____

OPTION TWO

I would like to subscribe to YOUTH**WORK** for 1 year *(12 issues)* and pay by cheque or credit card
i) I enclose my cheque / Postal Order for £22.80* *(payable to Trinity Square Ltd)*

ii) Please debit my Visa / Mastercard for £22.80*:

Card No. ☐☐☐☐
☐☐☐☐
☐☐☐☐

Expiry date ☐☐ / ☐☐

Signed_____

If you have any enquiries or difficulties please phone 0181-942 9761 and ask for Subscriptions.

* These prices apply up to 1 April 1997. After this date prices may vary - phone 0181-942 9761 to check.

All prices are one year UK only. For overseas subscriptions please pay by credit card or sterling draft only. Europe £34.30*. Rest of the World £35.90*. Trinity Square Ltd is registered under the Data Protection Act 1984 and holds names and addresses for the purposes of mailing details of goods and services. Details on request.
☐ Tick here if you do not wish to receive mailings from other companies.

HBYY